Letting Go

From *lost* to *found* on a one-way ticket

MELISSA WORK

ISBN 979-8-218-14605-4 Paperback
ISBN 979-8-218-14988-8 Ebook

To my father,

*I am forever grateful that I was
chosen to be your daughter.*

Always and Forever,

Daddy's Little Girl

CONTENTS

Author's Note i

1: The Beginning 1

2: Takeoff 7

3: The fight for my father's life 19

4: Barcelona, Spain 31

5: Benidorm, Spain 41

6: Justice for my Father 55

7: Taking action 61

8: Leaving corporate America and dating my new boyfriend . . 73

9: Alfacar, Spain 85

10: One way ticket to the Mayo Clinic 89

11: Granada, Spain 101

12: Continued mistakes 111

13: Memories that last a lifetime 121

14: Reflection over the past few years 125

15: Claira, France. 133

16: Almalfi Coast 137

17: Ohrid, Macedonia 141

18: Albania 145

19: Time to travel alone 153

20: Bled, Slovenia. 161

21: The Sound Of Music 169

22: The moment I knew I was ready to come home. 175

23: The last conversation I had with my dad where
    he was coherent 179

24: Learnings from Dad, Summed Up in a List of Ten 181

25: Letter to Chad Cunningham 183

26: Letter to Bradley Morrison 185

27: The New Equilibrium 187

AUTHOR'S NOTE

My dream to embark on a solo trip for three and a half months through Europe and finishing my journey in Egypt began with a single circumstance—a surgeon operating on my father, which left him fully disabled. This led to my life unraveling into a series of unfortunate events. There was the evening I was sexually assaulted. The breakup with the one who got away. The quitting of my corporate job. Finding out my new boyfriend was cheating on me. And losing a dear childhood friend.

I started thinking about the New Year and what the New Year would bring, and it felt like more of the same—no satisfying work, worrying about my dad, bad dates. And then I realized that instead of looking at this as something bad, I could reverse it. I could see it as a chance to do something that I wanted to do. To travel! *This year will be different*, I thought. I didn't have any limitations, and that felt so good.

Some of the closest people in my life thought that I had gone mad; others cheered me on. I didn't want to leave my father, but I knew it was time to do something for me to heal my soul. Before my father's surgery, I was excited for what each new day brought.

This feeling is a longing I desperately wanted to experience within my bones—to find the humor in life again. This is the feeling I remembered years later when my life had grown into sadness. The feeling that made me believe that traveling across the world was the only way back to myself and the person I used to be.

I decided that I wanted to begin my travels on January 10. This gave me nine more days before I took off. I was already brewing with excitement, and it was time to prepare for my trip. Where first? Nordstrom Rack. I went straight to the sales rack. There were the cutest modest dresses, all on the same rack. Jackpot. I'd found exactly what I was looking for! It was at this moment I felt confirmation that this trip was meant to be. You may be asking yourself, "Modest dresses? Where in the world is she going?" My heart was calling for me to go to Egypt.

Why Egypt? Ever since reading *The Alchemist* I have dreamed of going to Egypt. I have wondered how it would feel to see the most intact and oldest of the Seven World Wonders (the Great Pyramid of Giza). I have dreamed of exploring one of the oldest and most beautiful lands of the world and pictured myself in the desert in a beautiful red dress looking at the Great Sphinx while imagining the beautiful souls who built this jaw-dropping statue over 5,000 years ago. I was ready to turn my dream into reality. I started reading about Egyptian culture. I watched YouTube videos, read travel blogs and short stories—you name it. Anything that was available I wanted to get my hands on so that I would be more prepared for my trip.

My mom called me every day before I departed. My mother, a worrier, was worried sick.

"Are you sure you are making the right decision? Traveling to the Middle East as a solo female traveler? Aren't you worried or even a bit scared?! Your father is ill and we will miss you dearly."

I tried the best I could to ease my mother's worries and let her know that I needed to do this for me. My mother asked why I couldn't go with someone. "I need to do this alone. I want to heal my soul," I said.

I reached out to the most important women in my life and thanked them for being part of my tribe and told them about my trip, and as I wrote, I decided to call it my solo "Eat, Pray, Love" trip. These women cheered me on. I received confirmation yet again that this spur-of-the-moment decision on the eve of New Year's was what my heart was calling me to do. I decided to drive to my parents' home to give them one last hug and tell them how much I loved them.

Due to new Covid restrictions, Egypt required that visitors take a Covid test within ninety-six hours of departing. I went to a local urgent care and took a PCR test on January 8, 2022. My flight was scheduled to depart on Tuesday, January 11. On January 10, 2022, I received a call from urgent care.

"You did test positive for Covid via the PCR test. The CDC guidelines call for a full five-day isolation. So based on my notes here it looks like you need to isolate for another day or two, and it is okay to end after that fifth day."

I felt like I'd had the wind knocked out of me—it reminded me of a memory: how I'd belly-flopped into Emigrant Lake during my senior year of high school. I started writing a list of people with whom I had been in close contact. I had just visited my parents in Medford, Oregon, over Christmas and was terrified that I may have passed it to them. Once I got through calling my list of loved ones and the emotions started to settle, I postponed my dream of traveling to Egypt.

I had used airline miles to purchase my ticket and felt fortunate that American Airlines refunded my miles due to Covid-19. I re-booked my ticket to leave on January 18, 2022. I scheduled a Covid test to be completed on January 15, 2022, so that I would be prepared for Egypt.

On January 15 I saw Marcus, a registered nurse. He stuck a Q-tip in my nose and let me know that I would have results within the next few days. I started to get excited again for the trip of a lifetime to heal my soul.

I heard a ding on my phone and saw that I had received an email from the clinic.

> *Hi Melissa, I hope all is well. I wanted to let you know that you have in fact tested positive for Covid-19. Don't worry, this can be normal. It is typical for people to test positive for Covid-19 for up to three months and not be contagious toward others. Please call me if you have any further questions.*
>
> *Regards,*
> *Marcus*

This news was devastating. It was heartbreaking not only because I was scared that I was still carrying this relatively new disease—but it was equally crushing because per Egypt's embassy guidelines, one must have a negative Covid test to enter the country.

I canceled my trip and was thankful once again that American Airlines refunded my miles.

I lay in my bed and barely left my room over the next two days. I felt depression lurking over me and couldn't help but think, *Is the universe telling me I shouldn't go on this trip?* As I lay in bed feeling sorry for myself, I thought about the power of positive thinking. I realized at this moment the universe was telling me that Egypt was not the destination I was supposed to begin my trip. I reviewed the embassy guidelines for other countries and saw that Spain allowed travelers to enter the country with a recovery certificate without needing a negative Covid test. It was at this moment I knew that my heart was calling for me to start my solo travels in Spain.

Now what I had to do was save!

My banking career had allowed me to purchase my first property at twenty-six. Back then, I was adamant about not paying a mortgage; therefore I posted an ad on Facebook and asked if anyone was looking for a room. I got several hits. Within the next two weeks I had three roommates. By August 1, 2017, we were all living under one roof at my first home, which had a bright yellow door on Harold Street. Some people called me cheap—they said if there's a way Mel can make money, she will do so even if it means making her home into a hostel. Other people called me wise. I prefer the latter.

The day before I left I decided to drive to my safe space: Multnomah Falls. It is a twenty-five-minute drive from my home and has the most beautiful and jaw-dropping waterfall. It was a typical cloudy day in Portland. My eyelids got puffy as I watched the waterfall.

In one day my life would forever change. I would be leaving my comfort zone, my safe haven, my home, and traveling across the world to an unknown location where I didn't know anyone, nor what to expect. The feeling was exciting and paralyzing at the same time.

I felt confident that I was making the right decision to travel across the world and heal my soul. At this moment I knew I was ready.

THE BEGINNING

My life started unraveling in late December 2017. My father fell over a protruding piece of rebar and broke his knee. My father, who had always been healthy before, called me, but his voice had a skip in it. "I fell. I need to have surgery and I'm worried," he said.

Over the next few weeks I talked to him every day and I felt this surgery would be okay. After the surgery, my father started having issues of back pain and he wanted to get it checked out.

"What do you think it is?" I asked.

My father said, "I'm not sure. I'm going to speak to Patricia and see what she recommends." Patricia was our family doctor who had cared for my father for over twenty-four years. Patricia recommended that my father speak to a neurosurgeon to see what he or she proposed. My father visited two neurosurgeons in our local hometown of Medford, Oregon.

"James, I highly recommend surgery," said Dr. Cunningham, a neurosurgeon. "I advise on having a lower spinal fusion, which is my expertise. If you don't have this surgery now, you risk your back getting much worse."

Finally my father decided it was best to move forward with Dr. Cunningham's advice.

I was upset to learn that my father's surgery was on a day I'd be in Sedona visiting a friend. My parents told me to go, that everything would be fine, but on April 21, 2018, the day after my dad's surgery, I woke up in a terrified state. My clothes were drenched. What was happening to me? I never have nightmares, and this one had been dreadful. I took a deep breath and realized I'd left the heater on. I got up to turn the heater off—and the first thought that raced to my mind was my father.

I jumped up and called the hospital, but to my shock, it was impossible to get in contact with Dr. Cunningham. Before my father's surgery he would call my dad frequently to recommend surgery, and now: crickets. I kept calling but had no luck. The administrative assistant continued to use the excuse that Dr. Cunningham was busy and would be reaching out to me shortly.

I waited. My mother brought my father home, and I figured things were better, but then on May 8, 2018, when I called my mother, her voice was shaking and sounded unfamiliar to me.

"Your dad is not doing well. I have been trying to call Dr. Cunningham's office but have not had any luck speaking to him. I don't know what to do. Your father has started to drop weight quickly," my mother said.

"I'm going to drive home. This isn't normal. We need to take Dad to the hospital," I said.

When I arrived at my family's home, things felt different. That once euphoric feeling I received running through the door felt like a lifetime ago. I walked slowly to the front door. My right hand trembled as I grabbed the handle and heard a creak. I took my first step inside and met my mother's eyes. There were dark circles underneath her eyes and her lips were trembling. My father was sitting on the oversized gray sectional with his shoulders hanging downward. My father did not make any attempt to acknowledge my presence and proceeded to look toward the floor. I realized I needed to act fast because whatever was happening to my father was not normal.

I walked up to my dad.

"Dad, what's going on?!" I asked.

My father didn't say anything.

"Dad!" I said.

My father continued to look straight ahead. I grabbed my dad by the shoulders. "Earth to Dad! Talk to me. Tell me something."

My father seemed like he was in a different universe. *Why won't he say anything? He must hear me.*

I started to panic. "Dad! Please say something! Anything!" I didn't realize I was yelling at this point.

My mother ran over. "Jesus, Melissa. Stop! Don't you see something is happening to your father! He doesn't want to be like this! Don't yell at your father!"

I got a lump in my throat and fell to my knees. I grabbed my father's legs—holding them in a tight bear hug and looked into his eyes. "Please, Dad. Say something. Say anything. Tell me what is happening. Please, Daddy." My voice was trembling and high pitched.

"Melissa, that isn't helping. Something is happening to your father that is not within his control," my mother said. My mother grabbed my back gently and started to rub my shoulders.

I was looking at my once strong-willed father, who I believed could do anything, and now he could barely move or speak. "Mom, can you prepare Dad a bag of clothes? I'm going to take him to the hospital," I said.

"I already have one packed," My mother said.

I knelt down to the ground to be level with my father and I looked into his eyes. "I don't know what's happening, Popa, but hang in there. We are going to get you help. You have my word," I said. My arms were shaking as I gathered my purse, cellphone, and jacket.

"Mom, I'm going to drive Dad to the emergency room. I'll let you and Dad out at the front of the hospital, then I'll find a parking spot," I said.

When we got to the hospital, my mother wrapped one arm around my father's shoulders and walked beside him carefully. I parked my vehicle in the visitors lot and hurried into the main entrance. My parents were waiting in the lobby.

"James, they are ready to see you," someone called.

My mom and I got up with my father and walked over to the patient room. We waited thirty minutes and then a doctor walked in.

"What seems to be the problem?" asked the doctor. He was tapping his foot and crossing his arms.

My voice started cracking and I hadn't realized that my hands were still shaking. "My father had a surgery two weeks ago and since then he isn't vocal and has barely been able to eat. My father doesn't know what is going on and is scared. We are all scared and want answers," I said.

The doctor continued to look around the room. "That is very odd. I would recommend you continue to watch your father to see if he starts getting better. If he doesn't, then you should bring him back," said the doctor.

"I'm very concerned for my husband. If you don't help my husband, he is going to die," said my mother.

My mother broke out in a cry. I hadn't seen my mother cry in ten years, since my oldest brother was diagnosed with schizophrenia. I wrapped my arms around my mother and stroked her hair.

"Doctor, with all due respect, something is very wrong. My father is losing weight quickly and we're mortified. My father was a healthy man before surgery and after surgery he has changed dramatically. I don't know if something went wrong during the surgery but whatever happened my father woke up a different man." My lip started trembling uncontrollably. I moved my arms to reach out to the doctor, as if this would help. "Please help him!" I pleaded.

The doctor didn't make eye contact and looked at the ground when he spoke.

"I see why you're upset, but there's nothing we can do. If things get worse, you can bring him back," said the doctor. The doctor turned his attention to speak to a nurse about something unrelated.

At this point I didn't know how much worse things needed to be to get my father help. My mother and I left the hospital with my father in tears. My shoulders hung low as I opened the passenger door for my parents. I stayed with my mother for two days to see what I could do to help my father get better. I had to return to work and I asked that my mother call me if my father got worse.

2

TAKEOFF

January 20, 2022

My alarm went off at the crack of dawn and it was hard to get my eyes open. I brought my arms up to stretch reaching them toward the sky and swung my legs over the bed. My neighbor offered to take me to the airport. I lifted my blue carry-on bag into the back of my neighbor's car. My neighbor reached her arm toward my lap and placed a small talisman in my palm.

"I want you to have this. It will protect you in case you are in a dangerous situation," said Alice.

I looked down at the beautiful pendant and started rubbing my thumb on top of it. "Thank you," I said.

As we approached the airport Alice got out of the car to grab my luggage. She used her right hand to grab the top of the luggage and left arm to pull it out and place it standing straight. I looked into Alice's eyes and fell into her arms. Alice looked surprised. I held on tight.

I was about to leave everything I knew and in this moment Alice was the most comforting piece of home. A part of me didn't want to let her go, but I did.

"Thank you so much for driving me to the airport," I said.

"Goodbye, sweetheart. Have the time of your life!" said Alice.

My mother was fully caring for my father. The doctors said that my father had reached his new normalcy and there was nothing else they could do for him. My father was walking and speaking in small sentences, which reassured me that he would be okay while I traveled but I was starting to regret my decision of leaving my father.

I walked into the airport holding the handlebar with my right hand. I heard a clickity clack as my luggage followed and I readjusted my Gray backpack. My first flight was to Dallas, Texas. I sat in the middle seat and brought my big puffy black jacket. I placed it in front of me and used it as a pillow. I placed my left cheek on top of it and rested my eyes. It worked perfectly. I secured a few hours of sleep. When I landed in Dallas I had a quick connecting flight. I tugged my blue luggage behind me as I leaped over three stairs at a time to make it to gate D4. My backpack flew left and right. "Last call for flight A95," said the agent. I grabbed my boarding pass from my back right pocket. "You made it with two minutes to spare!" said the agent.

I don't know if you believe in destiny but at this moment I did. I sat next to the nicest woman. Her name is Carly. Carly was going to New York to celebrate a friend's birthday and I told her about my plans of going to Spain to start my solo travels. "I lived in Madrid for four years from the age of twenty-four years old! I love

Spain. I have to tell you about all the Spanish customs before you go," said Carly. Carly and I talked the rest of the flight.

She told me to watch out for pickpockets. She told me to stand my ground at grocery stores because people will cut you off if you don't look serious. She told me the men loved to flirt and were very romantic. She told me I must try Spanish tostadas. We exchanged phone numbers and added each other on social media. As we said goodbye, I wished I had more time with her, but was thankful for the time we did have.

I walked to gate 5, which was my final flight to Barcelona. I sat on a chair and pulled out my Air Pods from my purse to pass by time before boarding began. I waited for everyone to board so I could scope out if I would be able to have my own aisle. The flight was empty. I sat in the third row toward the back of the plane and placed my backpack under the middle seat.

In roughly seven hours I would be arriving in Barcelona, Spain. I used my big puffy jacket as a pillow and placed my legs up on the seat. I wrapped the cotton blanket around my legs and closed my eyes. When I awoke I felt more alert. I pulled up Priceline. I booked a hostel called St. Christopher's Inn. I would be arriving at 8:30 am on Friday. I paid 12 euros a night to sleep in a dorm with seven other females. I had no plans after the hostel, which made me nervous and excited at the same time. Once I got off the plane I had to scan my QR code that I had downloaded before arriving in Spain and get my checked bag.

Everything went smoothly, and the people at customs were friendly. I walked to baggage claim and saw a suitcase that was overly packed and half way open. I saw a Spanish man looking at the bag with his mouth half way open as he turned to look at me and moved his arms upwards as he casually shrugged his shoulders. At that moment we were both thinking the same thing—we hoped our bags were not opened.

I saw a lady use all of her strength to grab the bag and to my astonishment she didn't look surprised by her bag being halfway open. She proceeded to put her bag along with her other suitcases. My bag came out shortly after. I pulled up my hostel on google maps to see what would be the easiest and cheapest way to take transportation to St. Christopher's hostel which was the bus. I paid 5 euros for a one way ticket and was off. I was squeezing my eyes shut, then opening them in an effort to stay awake.

I made it to the hostel forty minutes later. As I opened the door I felt a blast of warm air rush into my face. It was colorful, lively and I felt a warm tingle wash over my body. I heard an English accent ask if he could book an extra evening. There were people from all over the world sleeping under one roof. I met a woman named Hilary who told me to purchase a padlock to lock my stuff in the room. "They have them for sale downstairs and the three euros is well worth it," she said.

I started walking to Vodaphone to get a sim card so I wouldn't have to pay ten US dollars per day for data. I saw a common area with hundreds of pigeons. I heard laughter around me and a small boy shuffle toward the pigeons. I stood still to take in the scene. Dozens of pigeons opened their wings and flew toward the sky. I had pulled out my phone and captured this magnificent moment just in time.

I arrived to Vodaphone and it cost 12 euros to get a monthly phone plan. Not bad at all! I had brought a second phone that had been sitting in my night drawer over the last three years. Vodaphone put the chip in my second phone and I was able to connect my primary phone to it without changing my number. My next stop was the ATM. By this point it was 1:30 pm and I couldn't be more excited to get back to my hostel and rest. I climbed the ladder and crawled into bed #3. I grabbed the thin knitted blanket and moved it over my shoulders as I turned my body toward the left and allowed the blank wall to put me to sleep. I awoke several hours later and was shocked when I saw the clock said 8:30 pm. Two girls were chatting lively about their plans for the evening.

I moved my hand toward the fabric of the curtain feeling the soft cotton against the palm of my hand. As I slid the curtain back it exposed the series of bunk beds and two figures within five feet of me. One was wildly tossing clothes from her suite case to the floor while the other was sitting cross legged. "Oh my gosh! I had no idea someone was in there! Were you there the whole time?!" asked Katie.

My hair was in every direction but straight. I was wearing the same outfit over the last 24 hours which was a yellow sweatshirt and blue sweatpants. "I was! I flew in from Portland, Oregon, and traveled over twenty-four hours," I said.

Katie waved her hand across her body in a friendly motion. "Nice to meet you, I'm Katie!"

I looked toward my right and made eye contact with the second girl. Lily walked toward me and lifted her arm as I shook her right hand. "I'm Lily!" she said.

"Where are you girls from?" I inquired.

"I was born in Venezuela and am now living in Russia," said Katie.

"I'm from the Netherlands," said Lily.

My eyes were immediately drawn to a beautiful butterfly tattoo on Katie's neck that complemented her five foot, five inch athletic build and warm brown eyes. Katie was full of life and spirit. Lily had wheat-colored hair with a smile that displayed perfectly aligned teeth and an inviting face. The moment I met Lily I felt at ease. We started speaking like little schoolgirls.

"What brought you to Spain?" I asked.

"I love to travel! I arrived in Barcelona without any real concrete plans," said Lily. I was shocked when I found out Lily was on her own journey of discovery like me. I never thought my father's surgery would have gone awry; I learned that things cannot be planned, and this inspired me to travel freely.

"What are you guys doing this evening?" said Katie

"We have no plans!" Lily and I said in unison.

"Jinx," I said as I pointed toward her with my right finger.

"Would you girls want to come downstairs to grab food and drinks then we could go out for a night of dancing?!" asked Katie.

I was still feeling jet-lagged, but there was no way I was going to pass on this opportunity. I climbed down the stairs and unlocked my padlock with my right hand. I found my yellow dress and pulled it over my shoulders. Katie introduced us to her friend Peter. He was originally from Venezuela and was now acting in Barcelona.

Peter told us what brought him to Spain. It was amazing to hear everyone's stories and how our paths interlocked. We took off arm in arm to a dance club. Katie invited a student studying abroad from the United States that she had met earlier that day named Simon. Here we were an actor, an artist, a recent graduate, a student studying abroad and me—all at the same place at the same time. We had one thing in common this evening—we were all in Barcelona and ready to have a great time!

The music was bumping and I could feel it vibrate through my body. It was lifting me up along with everyone else in the club. The lights were dimmed and color strobes flashed erratically pulsating from every direction. I ordered a round of drinks for everyone and Katie taught Lily and I a new dance move. We were the three musketeers swinging our arms back and forth with claw hands as we grapevined across the floor in *Thriller*-like motions. As I felt the sweat dripping down my temple from the exertion the Bartender announced that the bar was closing. My head swiveled around and my eyes landed on the red neon numbers displaying that it was 1 am. Where did the time go?! I realized for the first time I was not expecting any romance with any of the guys I was meeting, I was not worried about my dating future and it felt liberating.

Lily and I decided to explore the city of Barcelona first thing in the morning. When we walked up to the Sagrada Familia I was awestruck. I couldn't help but realize the dedication that went into this architecture. The sun shined directly on to the façade and the cool breeze washed over me. I sensed that the holy spirit was blessing the land.

Lily and I departed Sagrada Familia and meandered through the winding Spanish streets toward the salty sea breeze beckoning us to its glistening shores. A ball flying over the net caught our attention and we noticed a volleyball competition happening. There were sexy-toned Spaniards in every direction. I watched in admiration as men were spiking the volleyball. We found a small spot of sand and knelt down to take a seat. The waves were crashing upon the sand which transported me back to a time when I would sit side by side with my father watching the vibrant colors of the sunset in the Dominican Republic and speak about life.

I told Lily the short version about my father's health declining after his back surgery. Lily and I were both in tears by the end of the story. I could tell Lily was mature for her age, which prompted me to ask a question that was on my mind. "What really brought you to Spain?" I asked.

Lily started rubbing her legs and looked down. I could see a small tear fall to the soft beige sand. "My little brother committed suicide last year. It motivated me to do what makes me happy, which is to travel."

I reached across and squeezed her hand.

We sat in silence and watched the waves hit the sand. The surfers were gliding down the barreling water as it crashed toward us. We started approaching the town. I saw a group of five guys break dancing. People started to circle around the guys and I was excited to watch the show. I saw true authentic break dancing. I had never seen it before and was delighted by the gravity defying techniques they were showing off on the cobblestone ground.

After seeing the Cathedral De Barcelona we decided it was time to head back to the hostel. On a typical day I am proud if I accomplish 10,000 steps. By the time we arrived at St. Christopher's we were at 21,000 steps! My body was changing, getting stronger, right along with my mind and feelings about my future. I was ready for change. I had been living for the praise from other people. I had a sense that I was starting to live for myself and the only validation I needed was going to come from within.

As we approached the hostel I saw a little girl holding a camera that reminded me of the camera my father bought me for an eighth grade graduation gift. My father had taken me on a trip to the Dominican Republic in July 2005, which is my mother's homeland country. My father drove me to a friend's home. His name is Santiago.

"I think Santiago's wife is making Sancocho tonight," my father said.

My father had joined the Peace Corps in the Dominican Republic in 1973. He fell in love with two gemstones called amber and larimar. My father met Santiago through his love for Amber and started purchasing amber from him. When we arrived at Santiago's home, it was in a very poor area. The house was barely standing. The floor was made of dirt and I could feel the solid earth below my feet. There was a room that Santiago's daughter Noelia shared with three siblings and a second bedroom that Santiago and his wife shared with their newborn child. The table was made nicely with a light on top of it that flickered. We were greeted with smiles and warmth. I met Santiago's daughter Noelia for the first time and she was in the 8th grade too. She ran toward me and threw her arms around my shoulders.

At the time my Spanish was not good and Noelia could only speak a few words of English. We used our body language to express ourselves and there was plenty of laughter. "I'd like you to bring your camera to Santiago's home," said my father. I placed my camera in my bag delicately. When I met Noelia I pulled my camera out of my bag slowly. Noelia's eyes glistened when she saw it. Noelia moved her hand out to ask for permission and I handed her my camera. She started to touch every angle in admiration.

As the night carried on Noelia and I tried to communicate the best we could with the language barrier. Noelia took many photos and showed me with her shoulders held high. "Mira," she said, I smiled back and gave a thumbs up. She couldn't stop grinning ear to ear as she ran around the home. "Melissa, we are leaving in thirty minutes," yelled my father from the room next door.

I looked at Noelia and her shoulders hung low. She held the camera and looked at it with a longing as she moved her small hands around each angle. I knew at this moment I wanted to give my camera to Noelia. I tapped Noelia on the shoulder and pointed to my camera. "Para ti," I said.

I'll never forget what happened next. Noelia moved her arms up and shook her finger back and forth.

I put my hand on her shoulder and squeezed it tightly. "Gift for you," I said as I wrapped my arms around Noelia's shoulders.

Noelia tried to hand me the camera and I shook my head left to right. "No please," I said.

Noelia's eyes started watering as she gave me a tight hug. I started to feel her shoulders shake as I wrapped my arms around her. My dad yelled from the other room. "Melissa, I'm leaving!"

My father and I walked to his beaten-down Toyota.

"How do you feel?" I smiled at my father and reached my arm to open the door.

My father patted me on the back and said, "I am so proud of you, my sweet daughter."

I looked at his eyes and swore for just one moment I saw a tear. He walked to the driver side of the truck and had a smile that could have been seen from a mile away. In this moment I learned that material items come and go but the feeling you get when you help someone can last forever.

3

THE FIGHT FOR MY FATHER'S LIFE

May 10, 2018

On Thursday, I drove back to Medford. My mother and I walked through the emergency room door with new determination. I held my head up high and walked with force. My father's life depended on it. There was no time to be timid or scared. I knew that this was my only shot.

"We can admit your father for a few days. I recommend that my colleague interview your father to see if it has something to do with mental health," said the doctor. The doctor held a rigid posture and spoke with a sharp tone.

I find it hard to believe that whatever my father was experiencing was related to mental health but felt relieved that a doctor would look into what was going on so that we could move forward from this horrible nightmare.

"James, can you speak to me?" the psychiatrist said.

My dad gave a blank stare to the psychiatrist.

"James, I hear from your family that you are a successful businessman," said the psychiatrist.

My father continued to stare into the abyss.

"I recommend keeping James here for a few days to do some observation. Is that okay with you, Mrs. Work?" asked the psychiatrist.

"Yes, that is okay," said my mother.

My mother and I stayed with my father for the next three days. I fell asleep on the living room couch and my mother slept with my father in their room. I kept waking up in the middle of the night nervous that something bad had happened to my father. I looked into the crack of the door to see my parents sleeping and walked downstairs to rest my eyes. The psychiatrist had diagnosed my father with severe depression and recommended that my father take antidepressants. Antidepressants take six weeks to kick in. The antidepressants produced no change in my father. As week three approached my father gazed off into space. My father started to have delusions. He shook his arms in an upward motion and spoke to someone who wasn't there. My father continued to drop weight.

My world was crumbling before my eyes, and there was nothing I could do about it. The doctors in Medford continued to say that my father was experiencing depression or a psychosis. None of this made sense to me. How can someone who has never experienced a mental health disorder experience it rapidly after undergoing an invasive surgery at sixty-seven years old? What happened the day of surgery that changed my father so profoundly? Was there a way to bring my father's health back?

I looked at my father sitting on the couch with his shoulders slumped. I knelt down and grabbed his arms gently. "Daddy, I am going to get you help. I am so sorry you are going through this. I promise that I will do whatever I can to get you help," I said quietly.

My father looked at me blankly and tears welled from deep inside and started to flow like a river.

It was time I updated my father's friends and extended family on what was going on. The only way I could do this was by updating his friends on Facebook. I started typing away. Maybe someone would have advice? My father's friends shared their condolences and sent thoughts and prayers. I fell to my knees and laid my arms and head on the ground and heard a deep cry come out of my stomach. My shoulders started to shake uncontrollably and I stayed in that position for several minutes. It was at this moment I began to pray. I looked up toward the ceiling with my hands straight in front of me and yelled out to the Lord: "If you hear me, please help my father. He is the best man I know," I said. I put my forehead toward the floor and let it rest. Praying to the Lord provided me comfort and I needed it more than ever right now. I was in need of a miracle.

We next brought my father to Providence Hospital in Portland, where he was admitted. I was hopeful that the doctors would tell us what was going on with my father so that we could get my father back to normal. Instead the nurses placed a tube in my father's nose and taught my mother and me how to manually feed him.

"We believe what your husband is going through is severe depression," said the doctor.

"There's no way what my father is going through is depression!" My voice started to rise as my body trembled. "He had an invasive surgery and when he woke up he was a different man! Can't you call Chad Cunningham to find out what happened in that operation room?" I pleaded.

"We can only treat the symptoms of what your father is experiencing, and we believe it to be depression," said the doctor. The doctor yawned as he looked at his clipboard.

"Then why isn't he getting better after taking antidepressants? It has been over six weeks. Also, if he is depressed, why would he need a tube in his nose?" I asked.

My mother stood up tall. "Doctor, with all due respect, my daughter and I know my husband, and we know this is not depression."

The doctor raised his voice. He emphasized my mother's name as he spoke in a condescending manner. "Mrs. Work, with all due respect, I am the doctor and it's my job to diagnose your husband. This is what my diagnosis is."

My mother and I felt defeated. At this point we had been at Providence for a month and a half and had seen no sign of improvement in my father. A new doctor came into the room and spoke to my mother and me. The doctor reached for my shoulder and held it softly. "We do not know why there was such a significant change in your father after surgery," said the doctor.

"There has to be something that went wrong in the surgery," I pleaded.

The doctor shrugged her shoulders as she looked into my eyes. "I can simply answer what I am seeing right now, and we do not know what it is," the doctor said.

My mother raised her arm and raised her voice. "Please, there must be something you can do. A test? Something to find out what we can do to help my husband," said my mother. My mother turned her back away from the doctor and I could see her shoulders move as she covered her face with her hands. The doctor spoke quietly as the next words came out of her mouth. "There is nothing more we can do. I am sorry to be the bearer of bad news," said the doctor.

I put my hand on my mother's back. "If they don't want to help us, then we will go to another hospital," I said. I looked back at the doctor and made eye contact. "Thank you for your time," I said. I looked back at my mother and noticed how much she had aged. There were several new wrinkles on her forehead and she looked like she hadn't slept in weeks. "We need to take Dad back to Oregon Health and Science University. Hopefully this time they will admit him," I said.

My mother and I took my father to OHSU and they admitted him. I spoke to the same doctor that had declined us initially. The doctor made a comment that my father looked more frail. The doctor recommended getting a psychiatrist and neurologist involved within my father's care. The neurologist called me at 6 pm and let me know that my father had experienced a stroke during surgery or after surgery.

"There will be many more tests to come, and lots of recovery needed," said the neurologist.

I felt relieved. I was thankful to know what my father experienced so that we could start working on the path to recovery. My father walked his first steps in three months. I held his left arm tightly and saw determination in his eyes. My father continued to walk all the way to the front of the hospital.

The doctor informed me that they thought that there was something else going on with my father outside of the stroke. My dad was still unable to eat, drink, swallow, and could only speak a few words. I stayed with my father every night, and on October 22 I heard great news. A few doctors and psychiatrists thought that what my dad had been going through was called medical catatonia. A rare diagnosis.

Catatonia involves a lack of movement and communication. The doctors gave my father a medication called Ativan. Ativan is a tranquilizer. In patients with catatonia, Ativan is supposed to have the opposite effect of a tranquilizer, and it started to work. My father started to talk and eat. The nurse was able to remove my father's tube, and my dad started eating by himself. The doctors couldn't answer why my father had developed medical catatonia, but they thought they could get him back to baseline.

After my father started doing better he was admitted into the Marquis Rehabilitation Center. My father had physical therapy, speech therapy, and cognitive behavioral therapy. I would work during the days and stay with my father in the evenings. When my father started doing better, my mother went back to Medford to take care of my oldest brother, who was enrolled in a program that specialized in helping people with schizophrenia but the program had recently ended. I told my mother to help my brother and that I would be with my dad.

My mother had this idea. She wanted my father to go to her homeland: the Dominican Republic. He'd have a swimming pool for physical therapy and a nurse. My mother would be able to get help for my oldest brother, as it was too much for her to be a full time caregiver for two people.

"You guys would be so far, though," I said.

After several more conversations my mom was off to the Dominican Republic to get things ready for my dad. I took one week of vacation and brought my dad to the Dominican Republic. I met my father's physical therapist and speech therapist. My father would be in good hands and I felt at peace when I went back to the United States. My phone started ringing, and I saw that my middle brother was calling.

My brother recommended that I get an attorney to see if we could get answers for what happened to our father. I decided to move forward with his advice. I found an attorney named Mr. Wilson. His firm represents regular everyday people and has won many cases that served the public interest. I called Mr. Wilson's office and he agreed to meet with me on April 16, 2019.

I had never met an attorney before. I liked the feeling of his office. I noticed a lot of books—some were a few that I had read in the past and I remember feeling at ease. I told Mr. Wilson my father's story. I started with my father falling over the protruding rebar, how an ambulance picked him up and that my father needed to have knee surgery. After my father's knee surgery he started having back pain and met a neurosurgeon who recommended a complicated spinal fusion surgery.

"I'll take your case," Mr. Wilson said firmly.

The tension in my body left. I raised my hand to shake Mr. Wilson's and smiled from ear to ear. It was the first time I felt a sense of relief. I knew if my father was in good health he would be proud of who I chose to represent him. Mr. Wilson let me know that he would reach out to a third party anesthesiologist to see if there had been any wrongdoing during the operation.

Anytime I heard a buzz, I would check my email and it would be spam. I checked my email multiple times throughout the day. The anticipation was overwhelming. I woke up in the middle of the night to check my email knowing subconsciously that Mr. Wilson would never email me after business hours but on the off chance he did I wanted to be the first to see it. I would soon find out answers that I've been desiring all along. I wanted the truth to come to light in hopes that there was a treatment to help my father regain his health.

I had my air pods in and was lying in bed when the phone rang. I looked down and saw that I received an email from Mr. Wilson. The email informed me that the third party anesthesiologist did not find any wrongdoing during the surgery. I glanced over this email quickly then read each word diligently. I threw my phone across the room. I lay on my bed face down and sobbed. Crying had become a usual routine for me these days, and I didn't know how much more my body could take.

I wanted justice for my father but every corner that I searched came up empty. Mr. Wilson told me that though he knew this may be disappointing, there were a number of statements about my father's condition, when he declined and whether you and your Mom thought it was because of the back surgery. Finding that the anesthesia in the back surgery caused the later decline was a long shot, and I think Dr. Halmond's opinion puts it to rest. We need to direct our full attention to the knee injury and its consequences."

I agreed with Mr. Wilson that the best option would be to focus on the initial fall that had subsequent consequences. My father started eating but needed full time care. The doctors told my family that this was our new normal and they were sorry that they couldn't give us better advice. I was devastated. I tried to grow accustomed to my new normal but felt heartbroken. I missed the sunny days when I could call my father on a moment's notice and speak about life. I missed running into my father's arms after a breakup and hearing him say "Everything will be all right, honey." I missed the gross sandwiches he would make with mustard and cold cheddar cheese.

I gained thirty pounds and stopped talking to a lot of my friends. I would go home after work, hit the light switch, and snuggle deep inside of my sheets. I didn't want to see anyone or anything. I didn't want to hear a sound that could be the bearer of bad news. I didn't want to think about how scared my father must feel with his new reality. I wanted my mind to stop racing and to be blank like the sight I saw in front of my eyes when I held the sheets over my head.

The person who stayed by my side was Quincy. I met Quincy in August 2012 when I was twenty-one years old.

"Congratulations on your promotion to assistant branch manager! I'm excited to work with you!" said Quincy. Quincy was tall with a welcoming smile. He had a sense of humor that is larger than this world. He always had a joke behind his sleeve that would make others laugh when they needed it most. After the first week of working with Quincy, we became best friends. Quincy would even watch Lifetime Movie Network with me! We talked about the most random things and laughed until our stomach's hurt.

We took a road trip to California to visit a few of my best friends for a weekend getaway, and all of my friends asked me, "Why the heck aren't you guys together?!"

At the time I would answer that we were best friends and we both liked it that way. As the years went on our friendship continued to grow closer. Quincy is a Cancer and I am a Scorpio. For those of you who research zodiac signs, that is the BEST compatibility for my sign and I was well aware of that! A few years after college Quincy moved to Bend, Oregon, and I moved to Portland. One evening in 2017 Quincy was training in Portland for work and asked if we could get sushi. I hadn't seen Quincy in years and couldn't wait to catch up. The evening that Quincy and I got sushi, things felt different.

Quincy brushed my hand while grabbing a drink and I felt butterflies in my stomach. My face got warm as I looked toward the ground. "Is everything ok?" asked Quincy. At this moment I realized I looked at Quincy as more than a friend. We had an amazing dinner and when I was getting ready to say goodbye, I could tell he didn't want to leave my side.

I went back to Quincy's hotel and we started to watch a movie on Lifetime. It was about a nanny sleeping with the boss and the wife finding out. I was starting to get into it when Quincy looked into my eyes and I could see that his mouth was quivering. "I really like you," said Quincy. Quincy grabbed the back of my hair and went in for a kiss. I kissed Quincy and felt electricity ring through my body.

After that evening Quincy and I became attached at the hip. Quincy continued to live in Bend but would visit me every other weekend and I would visit him the weekends he didn't visit me. On April 14, 2017, Quincy asked me to be his girlfriend. Quincy and I explored Oregon in his black Toyota Tacoma. We would try new restaurants and find the humor in the silliest things. I felt like this was my person and everyone else agreed, especially my dad.

On February 5, 2018, I pulled up to my parents' home. My dad was outside speaking on the phone. He hung up and gave me a big smile as I ran into his arms. "Where's Quincy?" asked my father. "He has a few projects he's working on so I decided to come alone!" I responded. "When you get inside I want to talk to you about Quincy," said my father. This made me nervous. My dad has never wanted to talk to me about any guy I dated. I really like Quincy and cared about my father's opinion. We walked inside the house. I spotted my favorite painting and sat underneath it. Everyone knew this was my spot.

"I don't want you to be nervous, but I do want to ask you a question." My father looked at me, concentrating on my every move. "How serious are you about Quincy?" asked my father.

"I really like him. Why do you ask?"

"I like him, too. It's not often that you find a great guy," said my father.

Not only did I see how special Quincy was, but my father did too. Quincy's father worked in construction and his mother had a small daycare center. They have been married for over thirty years and the love they demonstrated reminded me of my parents. I couldn't have picked a better family to be a part of and felt blessed for the memories we were creating.

4

BARCELONA, SPAIN

January 23, 2022

I tried my first sangria in Park Guell. The sangria had a refreshing taste. I knew at this point sangria was going to be my drink of choice. Lily and I walked to the viewing area. The view was stunning. Every photo we took looked like an Instagram dream. My heart started to skip a beat, and a smile was erupting from my mouth. "Do you want to walk to the top?" Lily asked. As we were walking, I started panting and sat down on the cement arch.

I recognized the sick feeling I was having.

It was three years ago. A coworker had asked me out for drinks on September 5, 2019. Quincy and I had just broken up again, but we were still living together. I thought this was a bad idea—since I was still living with Quincy, but my coworker was so handsome, and so talented. I wanted to run away from all of my problems and go on a date with a man who was considered to be one of the most handsome bachelors at work. I rummaged through my room to find my cute blue top that shaped my body perfectly, black heels, and my nice fitting pants. We planned to meet at 6:30, and I didn't get off work until 5:30. I grabbed the wheel tightly as I was racing home to beat the clock. *Where is my black sweater?* I thought. I threw a few jackets on the ground trying to locate my favorite sweater—the one that made me feel confident. I grabbed my eyeliner and looked into the mirror as I put a perfect line over both of my eyelids. I walked down the stairs in my black heels and went straight for the kitchen. I looked at my watch. *Oh no*, I thought. It was already 6:20 pm—I did not have time to eat, as we'd planned to meet in ten minutes.

I pulled in and found a parking spot right in front of the bar. Score! I looked at the clock and it was 6:28 pm. *Right on time!* I thought. I looked at myself in the rearview mirror and took a deep breath: in and out. My palms were sweating and I readjusted the top of my pants before I swung my legs out of the car. I fidgeted with the door at the entrance of the bar and grabbed the handle with force to get it open. I tripped over my footing and looked up to see Bradley's big blue eyes. He smiled from ear to ear and I saw a dimple appear. *He is so handsome*, I thought.

"I ordered us a round of drinks," he said.

"Are you ordering food?" I asked.

"I already ate dinner," he said. I knew I should eat because I hadn't eaten since lunch, but I didn't want to eat alone since Bradley already ate. "Are you still dating that one guy?" Bradley asked. His voice sounded confident but his eyes gave him away.

He looked at me diligently as the words came out of my mouth. "No we broke up," I said as I looked down. Bradley blushed and reached for my hand.

"I am sorry to hear that," he said. My face started to feel warm.

"When was your last relationship?" I asked.

Bradley started to chuckle as we made eye contact. "Why do you want to know?" he asked.

"I'm just trying to make conversation," I said.

Bradley waved to the bartender to get us another round of drinks. I started to have fun and remembered the old me while we were getting drinks and getting to know each other outside of the work setting. It felt nice to flirt with a new man and forget my problems for one evening. Bradley waved to the bartender to get us another round of shots. I started feeling tipsy but the drinks felt so good hitting my lips.

"Do you want to go to the bar next door?" asked Bradley.

I nodded, and he grabbed my hand. I felt a spark dash through my body and looked up into his eyes where he met mine. I saw a grin appear from his lips.

Is this real life?! I thought.

He tugged my hand and I followed. "Can we get a round of tequila?" he asked the bartender. I haven't drunk shots in a long time, but I didn't want to look like I couldn't handle it.

I started to feel dizzy. Very dizzy. This was not normal for me. I fell over and Bradley caught me in a nick of time.

"I can order an Uber and we can go to my place so I can take care of you," said Bradley. I looked into Bradley's eyes and saw that he genuinely looked worried. "I should get home, I'm not feeling the best," I responded.

"I insist. What type of man would I be if I let you go home like this," said Bradley.

Bradley wrapped his arm around me and I stumbled a few feet until I saw the Uber.

"Please make sure she doesn't throw up," said the Uber driver.

"I got it," said Bradley. Bradley held my arm as we got out of the Uber, and I started throwing up outside his home. I couldn't stop. I felt Bradley's arm rubbing up and down my back as I continued to dry heave the last droplets of tequila that were in my body. This is the last thing I remember until the middle of night when I woke to Bradley on top of me.

When I realized what was happening, I said, "What the hell are you doing!"

Bradley stopped and lay next to me. "I'm sorry; I can stop," he said.

My stomach turned upside down; it was 3:40 in the morning and I couldn't believe I had just had sex with Bradley when I was not in my right mind. I tried to sleep but couldn't. I lay there with my mind racing, looking at Bradley as he turned to his side and slept peacefully. I eventually fell asleep to wake up to Bradley touching me at 6:40 am. I was dizzy and not really there. I didn't know what I was doing.

We started having sex. "Do you want a boy or girl?" Bradley asked. I didn't understand his question but he kept going. He asked again louder, "Do you want a boy or girl?"

I realized that Bradley wanted to cum inside of me. I wasn't on birth control and I realized how dangerous this was. Bradley wasn't wearing a condom. "Do not cum in me. I am not on birth control," I said.

Bradley nodded. "I won't," he replied.

I could tell Bradley was about to cum. I used whatever strength I had to push him off me, but it was not enough. He pulled me in close and pushed into me as deep as he could and came inside of me.

I pushed him off and yelled, "Why did you do that?! You promised me you wouldn't!"

"I was in the moment," said Bradley. I got up from the bed, threw my clothes on and left. I ordered an Uber to get back to my car; it was 7:30 am.

I called my best friend and told her everything that had happened. She let me know that it sounded like I got raped, but I brushed it off. How could this happen to me? I was twenty-eight years old—seasoned at dating and had just had the most violating sexual experience of my life. My brain was scattered—I didn't know how to process all of the emotions I was experiencing. I pulled my car up to my home and saw that Quincy's truck was still in the driveway. *Why isn't he at work?* I thought.

I tiptoed up my carpeted stairs and went straight to the shower. I threw off my clothes and turned the hot water on.

I let it sit for several minutes before I got in. I grabbed the bar of soap next to the sink and sat cross-legged in the shower. I started to choke and I heard an unfamiliar sound come out of my mouth. I held my mouth with my hand and bit down until I saw a stream of blood go down the drain with the water. Streams of water started to flood my eyes. I started rubbing the soap bar with all my strength against each part of my body. I stood up and began rubbing some more. It started to hurt. I looked at my body in disgust. I felt dirty. I felt gross. How could I leave this shower and look Quincy in the eyes? I had to get myself together. I needed to be at work in less than an hour.

When I got out of the shower I saw that Quincy had left for work. I felt a moment of relief for the first time. I dried myself off, put on a white professional top with black slacks and a cardigan grabbed my work keys and rushed out the door. When I got to work I acted as if nothing was wrong. My mind continued to race at a million miles per hour and I wanted to turn it off. I heard a ding on my phone and saw that Bradley had texted me. I turned my phone over and checked emails. During lunch I texted Bradley back. *Maybe I can pretend like last night never happened. Maybe this will all go away*, I thought.

I started therapy—and saw a psychiatrist. I couldn't concentrate. I started taking Adderall for the first time to help me concentrate. I had taken Ativan after my father was prescribed it and knew it could make me feel like a zombie. I started taking Ativan to remove the anxiety I experienced when I saw Bradley at work. The Adderall caused me not to sleep, and my doctor then recommended sleeping medications. I was a zombie strung out on drugs. This is the first time in my life that I took any drugs and or medications, and the only thing that numbed me from my pain.

After this experience I pursued Bradley. I knew subconsciously that everything about this was wrong. I felt violated, I felt ashamed and felt like I'd lost all of my self-respect. I felt that the only thing that would make this better was if I was with Bradley—so that this rape had meaning and maybe wasn't a rape at all? Bradley showed a lack of interest that made me want him more. I realized what an unhealthy cycle this was but didn't know how to move forward in a healthy manner. Bradley and I had consensual sex soon after that first time. Afterward I felt awful. I knew that I'd been violated beyond words the first evening and needed to get away from this individual to begin to heal.

I told Quincy what had happened. Quincy asked that I report Bradley to the police. He was adamant. "Dammit, Melissa, you were raped! Fucking report him!"

"It's not that easy!" I yelled. "I was drinking, he was drinking. I should have never gone out. Then I slept with him a second time, consensually. What the fuck is wrong with me?" I put my head in my hands as my shoulders started to move uncontrollably.

Quincy moved out. I wanted to talk to someone but felt so ashamed. I wanted to tell my dad. He always knew what to say, but now I had no one. I had to deal with this head-on and the only way I knew how was by taking drugs prescribed to me by my doctor. On January 29, 2020, I pulled out my phone and texted Bradley: "I want to take you up on your offer of transitioning to a different location. I would feel more comfortable at work. Let me know when you're able to accomplish this. Thanks."

Now, I took a deep breath and brought myself back to the present. My shoulders hung low and started to shake. Lily grabbed my shoulder firmly and wrapped her arm around me. She wiped a tear away from my cheek. We took a bus back to our hostel shortly after. Lily went out and I decided to stay in and gather my thoughts.

I awoke to a text from my mother at 5:34 am. "I think I got it last Sunday when I was doing work at one of the rentals. Last night your dad was complaining of aching muscles. The doctor told me not to take him for a test since I tested positive."

Now the fear started to kick in. I was sitting in my top bunk bed. The room was filled with seven other girls and it was 5:34 am. I left my hostel and went to the shower to call my mom. A quick pain skipped through my stomach and up the right side of my chest.

A million questions started racing through my mind. *How is my mother really doing? Did my father get Covid? Are my parents going to make it?* My dad was seventy years old and my mom was sixty-five years old—they are considered high risk and you already know the condition my father is in. I arranged for Ann to bring my parents groceries. I could go back in the direction I came from or I could trust that my parents were going to be ok and continue to move forward as I planned. I got back to my bed at 6:30 am. I couldn't fall back asleep. There was too much on my mind. My worst nightmare had become reality, and I was across the world in Barcelona. I wanted to listen to my mother's words and believe the confidence she projected, but I also wanted to be close in case something happened.

As soon as Lily woke up I told her what had happened. "My mom tested positive for Covid," I said.

Lily looked at me with care in her eyes. "Think positive thoughts. Your parents are strong and resilient. If your mom needs you she will let you know," said Lily. Lily squeezed my shoulder and reassured me that my parents would be fine.

5

BENIDORM, SPAIN

January 24, 2022

Lily and I left our hostel at 9 am to head to Benidorm, Spain. Once we got on the bus I felt exhausted. I thought I would be over the jet lag by now but the lack of sleep and finding out my parents got Covid didn't help. I found a row that was empty, took off my large puffy jacket, and slept. I looked at my cell phone and saw that it was 11:30 am. I felt like a new woman when I woke up. Lily and I had to transfer buses but would be at our final destination a few hours later.

The stars were sparkling as I pulled my jacket sleeves over my hand. We walked along the road until we reached her car. "How long has it been sitting here?" I asked.

"A few months," said Lily.

"Do you think it will start?" I asked. Lily and I were both pleasantly surprised when the car started. We squeezed our suitcases into the car and were off to Benidorm, Spain.

"What happened after you asked Bradley to move branches?" asked Lily.

Bradley never responded to my text.

On February 5, 2020, I started setting up for the gala. I was taking attendance and giving each employee a goody bag. "Thank you for being one of the first attendees to arrive at the gala! This is a token of our appreciation," I said. I scanned the attendance list one last time and was relieved when I didn't see Bradley's name on it. I saw Bradley's best friend and coworker walk through the door. My heart started beating faster and I gritted my teeth. "Thank you for being one of the first attendees to show up to the gala. Here is a gift," I said.

His friend gave me a gentle smile and looked kind. *I wonder if he puts on an act, too?* I thought. Thirty minutes later I turned around and saw Bradley behind me slurring his words and speaking loudly. *How did he get into the event?!* I thought. Bradley looked at me and smirked. My hands started trembling as I tried to gain my composure.

I continued to hand out the rest of my goody bags and made it a point to look straight.

Bradley rubbed his shoulder against mine. "My bad," he said.

I looked the other way and took a deep breath. My therapist taught me that breathing can make the world of difference and I prayed that in this moment it would work. My manager got on stage and I heard my name called. My peer tapped my shoulder and said, "Congratulations, Melissa! Get up there!" I was already shaking from seeing Bradley, but now I was shaking as I walked up to the stage to accept an award.

"It is no wonder that Melissa is receiving the 2020 Culture Advocacy Award. Melissa is one of the hardest workers—"

Suddenly a large commotion broke out. I looked toward the audience and saw Bradley laughing with a group of bankers, advisers and managers. For a split second Bradley and I made eye contact, and he motioned his arms at me and continued to laugh.

"Please be quiet, and give your attention to Mr. Wilson," shouted my regional director.

I felt like my body was about to collapse. I held whatever pride I had left as I stood in front of hundreds of my peers on stage. I gave my manager a hug and accepted the award and walked back to the attendance table.

After the awards ceremony, one of my fellow branch managers tapped my shoulder. "Are you all right?" she asked.

I looked at her and forced a small smile. My eyes started to water. "I overheard Bradley saying sexually explicit comments but could not hear the exact words," she said.

"Thank you for letting me know," I responded.

"Congratulations on your award! It was well deserved!" said another peer.

"Thank you," I responded weakly.

My shoulders hung low as I picked up last-minute items. "Is there anything you need help with before I take off?" I asked.

"No you've done enough! Get out of here and enjoy your award!" responded my peer.

I walked out to my car. My right hand was shaking as I pulled out my key. I pressed the top button and opened the door as quickly as I could. I grabbed the steering wheel and realized that my knuckles were starting to hurt. I let out a yelping sound from the inside of my stomach and started to breath fast.

I felt like my heart was going to jump out of my chest. I dialed my friend's phone number. "Can you please come over?" I pleaded.

"What the hell is going on?" Alexandria asked.

"It's a long story but I'll explain everything when you get to my place. Please hurry," I said as I hung up the phone. I pulled into the driveway and saw that Alexandria was in a car with her friend. She got out of the car and I ran into her arms. I was hyperventilating at this point and couldn't get a word out of my mouth.

Alexandria started stroking my hair and rubbed my back. "It's going to be okay. I'm here now," she said.

Alexandria wrapped her arm around my shoulder and helped me walk inside my home. I kicked off my heels and took off my dress as Alexandria guided me to my room. I dropped my award on the ground.

"It's Bradley isn't it?" asked Alexandria.

I nodded my head as a tear fell to the ground.

"You don't need to say anything more," she said.

I cuddled up in bed and Alexandria wrapped her arms around me as if she was a polar bear and I was her cub. I cried into the sheets as Alexandria stroked my hair.

"Can you rub my back?" I asked. Alexandria started to rub my back with her fingertips and I relaxed my eyes.

"You don't deserve this," she said. I rested my eyes and it was lights out.

I woke up feeling forty pounds heavier. It was time to attack this head-on. At 8:30 am I pulled out my phone and texted Bradley. "I'm assuming that you're working on the transfer on your end, otherwise I'll have no choice but to speak to John about getting a new Partner to cover my branch. I would rather this be amicable between you and I and not involve upper management. You don't have to worry about me discussing our conflicts. I will respect your privacy. Please give me an update as I've waited patiently over one week, and it's important that we both feel comfortable in our work environment," I said.

I saw a ding on my phone. My heart stopped for a moment as I took in the words, "I'm not requesting a transfer. I don't control the advisor territories, nor does John. That is Carter's wheelhouse. Perhaps you should look toward getting comfortable or transferring branches," said Bradley.

It was time I put my big girl pants on and call my manager. Unfortunately, this is much easier said than done. My feet shook as I walked to the back room. My stomach ached and I felt like I could throw up at any moment. I pulled up my contacts and searched for John. I hit the green button and held the phone to my ear. The ringing felt like eternity. I could hang up now and continue to avoid this issue. "Hello," said John.

Too late, I thought. "Do you have a moment?" I asked. I could barely contain my voice.

"What can I help you with?"

I let my manager know that I would like a partner change due to the lewd comments directed toward me at the gala by Bradley. Furthermore, I informed my manager that a traumatic event happened outside work where I felt violated, and that I did not feel comfortable or safe working with Bradley.

"Is it possible for Bradley to not hold appointments at my branch while Human Resources conducts their investigation?" I asked.

There was a long pause. I was rubbing my pant leg with anticipation. "This isn't possible until Human Resources finishes their investigation," said my manager.

My voice cracked. "I am disappointed to hear that," I responded.

I spoke to my doctor and started a leave of absence on March 2, 2020, as it grew to be unbearable to work in the same office space as Bradley.

"Why are you taking a leave of absence?" asked my manager.

"I am going on a leave of absence because of the traumatic event that happened with Bradley outside of work, and because of the sexual comment lobbied at me at the gala. It was the most humiliating experience of my life, and I do not want to continue to work in an environment where I do not feel comfortable or safe," I said.

My phone started ringing and I saw that it was my manager. I took a deep breath in and out clicked on the green button.

"Hello, Melissa. I wanted to let you know that Human Resources concluded their investigation and Bradley will not be covering your branch any longer," he said.

I smiled from ear to ear. "Thank you for letting me know!" I responded. My eyes started to water as I wiped the tears away with my hand. I returned to work feeling stronger. My mind felt clearer. I received a call from Human Resources and the representative assured me that Bradley had been reassigned from my branch and would not be working in the same office space as me. I felt relief and a smidge of happiness for the first time in a long time. My life was starting to look up!

Lily squeezed my hand. "It was resolved, then?" she asked.

I shook my head. "I wish it had been that simple," I responded.

The city had many skyscrapers. Lily parked her vehicle on the side street where there was free parking and we checked into our hotel. Lily and I discussed her previous relationships and were exhausted by the end of our conversation. I woke up feeling refreshed. Lily and I went to a cute café down the road. There were four tables that were filled with older happy couples that were soaking up this moment like us. The buildings were wrapped around the beach. There was a yellow hotel that had Villa Venecia written on the side that hung up on the mountain. I felt the sun hitting my face as I squinted my eyes to look at the waitress. It was refreshing to see how much Lily and I related. She was becoming one of my best friends that I felt like I knew for a lifetime.

"What happened after you returned to work?" asked Lily.

Covid-19 shook up the world—it also changed the dynamics of my corporate job. I was a branch manager inside of a grocery store. My bank decided to close most grocery store locations temporarily to stop the spread of Covid-19.

"The closure of Fred Meyer locations is a temporary decision to protect our employees and clients. We will have employees being shared among the branches that are open in the meantime," said senior leaders.

I was moved to a branch in North Portland. I looked at my phone and saw my manager was calling. "Hello, Melissa, I was wondering if you could help manage the downtown branch, as one of the employees has tested positive for Covid-19, and as a result the entire team has to quarantine."

I paused. "I guess that's okay," I said. When I hung up the phone, the emotions I tried to suppress started sweeping over me like a tornado.

The downtown location is the branch that Bradley worked at, and this triggered me. I had come so far within my mental health/peace and didn't want to disturb this. I looked up my recent call history and clicked on John's name and he answered after the second ring.

"Is there a chance you could have another manager cover?" I asked.

John paused.

"I am fearful of running into Bradley while covering for the branch," I said.

"You have my word that you will not see Bradley. He is on a mandatory fourteen-day quarantine, as he was exposed to Covid firsthand," said John.

"But—" I pleaded.

"I have to go, Melissa. I have other issues to tend to," responded John.

I covered the downtown branch from July 13 through 16. I looked down at my phone and saw that my manager was calling.

"Hi, Melissa! I wanted to let you know that I found a replacement to cover for you and take over tomorrow," said John.

I paused. "I appreciate you doing that. Bradley is the only human being that I do not want to be around. I never want to be placed in a situation where I feel uncomfortable and unsafe," I said.

"Understood," responded John. "You'll have to go to the branch to change keys and complete any branch tasks before she takes over."

On July 16, 2020, while I was completing compliance tasks with the replacement manager, Bradley came to the branch (six days after being exposed to Covid-19). Bradley gave me a smirk and greeted me while I completed ATM tasks with the incoming branch manager. My heart stopped. All the hard work I had done to help my mental health came undone. Panic flooded back like a hurricane, and there was nothing I could do to stop it. I took a deep breath and started counting to ten. "One-two-three-four—" My heart started beating faster, and I thought for a moment that I may have a heart attack. *Please let this stop. There are team members here. Control yourself, Melissa*, I thought. I left the bank as quickly as I could.

I got into my car and pulled out of the parking lot as I dialed John. My voice was shaking like everything else in my body, and I felt defeated. "Bradley showed up to the branch I just thought you should know," I said. I felt a pain above my left boob and started rubbing it gently. I pulled over to the side of the road and laid my head on the steering wheel. My heart continued to beat fast and I wanted to calm down. I took a deep breath in and out. I repeated this technique three more times, then I grabbed my purse and threw a 1 mg tablet of Ativan toward the back of my throat.

I felt the pain release from my body. I felt emotionless and numb. I started to drive back to the North Branch location. I was upset at John for giving me his word and letting me down, but wanted to give him the benefit of the doubt. I was sure he felt horrible about this situation and could not control what Bradley did. I spoke to my psychiatrist, who was just as outraged as I was. I started to meditate and try new techniques to help manage my anxiety. After a few weeks I started to get my groove back.

On August 21, 2020, I was sitting at my computer at work and thought I saw Bradley out of the corner of my eye. Bradley had indeed walked through the door. He made eye contact with me, gave me a smirk, and sat at the table behind me. My hands started trembling and then I realized that my knees were, too. I was losing control of my body. *Where's my Ativan?* I thought. I reached for my purse underneath the table. I grabbed two small pills and threw them toward the back of my throat. I didn't want to walk toward the water fountain. I was worried I would tumble over like a domino. I swallowed the pills with my own saliva. *Don't worry, Melissa. Soon you won't feel anything*, I thought. Sure enough, I started to feel numb.

I started to count to ten as I took a deep breath: *one-two-three-four-five.*

"Melissa, there is a client waiting to see you for your joint meeting with Charlie," an employee said.

"I'll be right there," I replied. I turned toward the client to wave to her and felt Bradley's eyes on my back. I didn't trust myself to walk over to the client as I was still trembling even with the excessive medication I had just taken. I walked to the private office, where I met Charlie and we sat down. Charlie made me feel calm and I turned my back away from the door so that I wouldn't look at Bradley again.

Once my joint meeting was done, I called John. "Bradley showed up to the branch. Why wasn't I notified?" I asked. My voice had started to rise into an aggressive plea.

"Maybe Bradley didn't know you were working at that branch?" John said.

At this point I started to grow hysterical. "A mutual client let me know that Bradley had informed him of my whereabouts only a few days ago! Why are you not listening to me?! I have been here for several months!" I said.

"I will discuss the situation with Bradley's manager. You have my word it will not happen again," said John.

Bradley had never held an appointment at the North Branch location before. Bradley had worked at JP Morgan Chase Bank for six years at this point, and this was the first time the other branch manager had seen him there. It was preposterous that my manager was making excuses for Bradley and continuing to jeopardize my mental health. I went into the bathroom and fell to my knees. I placed my head in my hands and my body started to shake.

"Are you ok in there?" asked David. David was the joint manager, and we had grown to be close.

"I'll be out in a few minutes," I responded. I gathered what strength I had, placed my hands on the cold hard ground, and picked up my trembling legs. I looked in the mirror and wiped the tears away with toilet paper. I splashed my face with water and dried my face off.

After work I got into my car and held the steering wheel tightly. I felt numb and overwhelmed at the same time. I got on the freeway to drive downtown. I had plans to meet with my friend this evening and had already canceled twice before. I looked at the Willamette River and saw the current taking a plastic bag. I wished at that moment that I could be the plastic bag that was floating along the river. I turned my head to face the freeway as a tear hit my right pant leg. As much as I hated feeling emotions, I hated the fact that I had to take Ativan to numb my pain and Adderall to concentrate. I was in a vicious cycle where my life was unfolding before my eyes and I didn't know who I was becoming. *Concentrate on the road*, I thought.

I was beginning my battle with pharmaceutical drugs. A battle that I never dreamed I would be in and a battle that is difficult to win. The system that encouraged an unnecessary surgery to my father that left him disabled. The system that prescribes multiple drugs to make an extra dollar while side effects could be more devastating than the problem itself. The system that was about to eat me alive if I didn't change my ways, but here I was becoming another statistic and hating myself even more because of it. I started to lose weight quickly. Adderall removed my appetite and I had to continue to remind myself to eat. The weight continued to fall off and people around me would compliment me. I would manage a smile as I replied by thanking them. The truth was I felt worse than I had in my life, and no one seemed to notice.

I drove to my safe place of Multnomah Falls. It started to sprinkle and I looked up at the sky. I fell to my knees and screamed. The scream shook my shoulders but there was nothing else in this world that could make me feel in touch with reality than screaming from the depth of my lungs. I let the rain hit my face as I looked up at the sky and screamed once more. "Please let this pain stop, Lord," I yelled. I let my head fall to the ground with my hands beneath it.

The next week I spoke to my psychiatrist.

"What the hell is wrong with your manager?!" she growled.

My voice was weak, and I felt like I could crumble at any moment. "He promised me it wouldn't happen again," I said quietly. That once strong woman was gone with everything else in my life.

"Are you doing ok?" asked Quincy.

I nodded my head. "Are you sure? You don't look the best," said Quincy.

I mustered strength to force a smile, but knew my eyes gave me away. "I'll be fine," I responded.

On September 1, 2020, I walked through the doors at 9:30 am and smelled cologne. I remembered that smell vividly. *Oh no, this cannot be happening again*, I thought. I turned around and saw Bradley right behind me. His shoulder brushed past mine as I walked into my peer's office and informed him that I would be leaving the branch. I turned around and walked to my car quickly. My legs were trembling, and I thought my knees might give out.

I texted my peer that I would come back to the branch once Bradley left. *Where the fuck is my Ativan?* I thought. *Oh no, I left it at the house.* I started to breathe quickly: *One-two-three-four-five. Why didn't I bring it?! Six-seven-eight.* I started hyperventilating. *I need Ativan right now!* I started to hold my breath. Tears flowed from my eyes and I wanted to scream. The emotions felt overwhelming. I cannot handle this. *Please make it stop. Please, Melissa, think. One-two-three-four-five.* I started to gasp for air. *Six-seven-eight.* My breathing started to slow and I felt my heart rate slowing down with it. I rushed home to take my Ativan.

Two hours later I received a text from David that let me know Bradley had left the office.

Now, I shut my eyes. I grounded myself. Here I was with Lily, and she was looking at me, her mouth a thin line. "I cannot believe your manager continued to allow this to happen. Is he still working there?" she asked. I nodded my head. Lily squeezed my shoulder and pulled me in for a hug.

6

JUSTICE FOR MY FATHER

April 21, 2021, was the day that my mom and I would be getting deposed from the opposition side. The deposition would be conducted virtually, and I wanted to make sure my mom didn't have any issues signing on, so I drove to Medford. I called the conference line at 9 am and saw a court clerk, Mr. Wilson, and an attorney named Paul for the opposition side.

The opposition attorney started his introduction, and the court clerk asked me to raise my right hand. I've never been through anything like this and had butterflies in my stomach—not the good kind. I knew Paul would be asking me a lot of questions. I met my mom outside of the room for lunch and made sure she was signed on. I had to go back to Portland, so I left my laptop with my mom. It broke my heart that in ten minutes my mother would have to go through the same process I had.

She has already been through so much with my father's health and my oldest brother's disability. My mother was now a full-time caregiver for two people. I felt protective. I didn't want any more pain inflicted on my mother but knew that she had to go through this process for us to be finished.

I grabbed my mother's shoulders and pulled her in for a hug. "Stay strong. This will be over shortly," I said.

I knew what would happen next would be mediation. On May 31, 2021, we would settle or go to trial. It was apparent that the insurance company would take ownership of the broken rebar that caused my father to break his knee, but the true question was how much ownership would the insurance company take? The real trouble started after my father broke his knee and started to have back pain. That is when the back operation was recommended which deemed my father fully disabled.

The only thing that connected my father's fall over the rebar to his back was Dr. Cunningham's documentation. "James Work could not stand up straight, was bent over at the waist after a month in bed for the knee and that his diagnosis was 'acute on chronic back pain.'" My father had never complained of back pain until he fell over the rebar. That horrible fall had a ripple effect of unfortunate events.

There was only one problem—although I thought this case should be easy to prove, we needed a doctor to connect the fall to my father's back surgery, and my father had only seen one primary care doctor over the last twenty-four years, whom I hadn't spoken to. My father's attorneys had worked their hearts out on my father's case, which they took on a contingency fee arrangement.

This boiled down to one factor. Would my father's primary care doctor connect the two? Mrs. Newberg called Dr. Patricia's office, and Dr. Patricia was open to speaking to her about my father's case. I could hardly think of anything else. As the minutes rolled by I tried to distract myself but couldn't. I got on my knees and I prayed.

"Lord, please give me some good news. Please allow us to prove this connection through Mrs. Newberg and Dr. Patricia's meeting."

I heard a ding on my telephone. It was from the attorney.

05/13/2021:

Hi Melissa,

I spoke with Patricia, MD, today. I explained the fall and the suit. She had not known about it. She has testified once in a med mal case for a patient. She takes testifying very seriously and looks with disfavor on frivolous or unsupportable cases. She sees this as a meritorious case and shared the opinions below.

She had her chart in front of her and so did I. We reviewed it and discussed her care of Jim over the years, including the time period after the fall up until her last care. She was candid and supportive and said:

She did not remember that he had fallen but her 1/3/2018 chart note documents the fall and surgery and his post-knee surgery onset of depression.

Her 2/28/18 chart note documents "He has had low back pain on and off throughout his life but after being immobilized for 5 weeks this really flared up. He has pain radiating down both legs at times and in the morning when he first stands up. He has numbness in both legs for about a half an hour." This supports her opinion below that the fall changed Jim's back condition.

She will testify with reasonable medical probability:

The fall was a "but for" cause of the patella fracture.

The fall was a cause of the need for back surgery under the previous infirm condition test. She added that a patella fracture (like a sternal fracture) is rather rare and requires a lot of force. In her opinion, the force was sufficient to injure his back and that injury could well have gone undetected or underappreciated because of the acute nature of the patella fracture. She noted that the findings on the March 13, 2018, lumbar spine MRI of spondylolisthesis and stenosis are not ordinarily trauma caused but the fall could have made what was previously no or low pain acutely symptomatic. She likely will discuss this with her psychiatrist brother to gain more insight into how a fall could make such conditions which prior were not or very low symptomatic into acutely painful ones. {We could consider consulting with him later but I don't think we need that level of input before mediation}

The fall was a cause of the changed mental state/catatonia which was very dramatic ("he was a changed man"), may be multifactorial but is so clearly related in time to the first and then second surgery, that, to her, causally related under the substantial factor test.

This was for her an "aha" moment: she had been surprised and a bit mystified at Jim's dramatic change from a rock to essentially an invalid. Looking at the string of events it is clear to her that the fall and surgeries utterly changed the patient she had known for 20 plus years as "the rock" of the family, supporting and caring for all of them, especially Richard. She added that if he had fallen in 2017 and the onset of his decline was in 2019 she would find it unrelated. However, with the timeline we have, it is clear to her that the fall, which led to the surgeries, was a "substantial factor causing his current condition."

Sincerely,
Mrs. Newberg

When I read this email, I fell to my knees. Finally there was proof between my father's back operation, his knee, and the devastating impact this made on his life. I wanted the truth to come out so desperately. The truth that I never realized would be so hard to get from the medical world.

Mediation arrived on May 31, 2021. Judge Boris facilitated. Judge Boris had a welcoming smile and oval eyes that looked sincere. I met Mrs. Newberg at her office and gave her a hug in person for the first time. "We're almost done," said Mrs. Newberg as she patted my back. Mrs. Newberg and I sat in her office and dialed into the virtual link.

Judge Boris explained the process and that she would be coming in and out of the room to discuss with the opposition side in hopes we could agree on a settlement. Judge Boris had a calm demeanor about her, which provided me comfort. This process started at 9 am and was expected to last until 5 pm.

"Would you like any water?" asked Mrs. Newberg. I nodded my head. Mrs. Newberg got me water and I drank it in one gulp. The nervousness had taken over me and I realized the last three years of pain and suffering had come to this day to see if I could get justice for my father. Mediation began and as morning turned into afternoon as expected the opposition wanted to take responsibility for the knee but not the back and its subsequent consequences.

"The opposition side has expert testimony that the back surgery was unnecessary and should have never happened," said the opposition attorney.

I didn't want to believe what I had just heard. A million thoughts started racing through my mind. If Dr. Cunningham hadn't performed this surgery, I would still have my person. My dear father. I couldn't believe I was finding out this surgery was deemed unnecessary three years after my father's surgery.

As the hours flew by I heard Judge Boris make a comment that referred to the anesthesiologist. "The defense brought up the anesthesiologist's prior record," said Judge Boris. By the end of the afternoon we came to an agreement as both sides saw it as a risk to go to trial. I was worried that there would be no justice for my father, so we decided to settle.

"This case is concluded," said Judge Boris. Mr. Wilson looked at the screen and Mrs. Newberg rubbed my back. I wrapped my arms around Mrs. Newberg neck. I was overwhelmed with emotion that this was finally over. Mrs. Newberg grabbed a Kleenex box. I blew my nose and tossed the Kleenex into the trash can.

7

TAKING ACTION

When I got home the evening of September 1, 2020, my eyes were heavy. My body ached from top to bottom. I lay on my bed as my mind paced quickly. *Will I ever have peace again? I wish I could talk to my father and get his advice so badly*, I thought. Now I felt like a loan sheep ready to be pounced by tigers. *What did your father teach you, Melissa? I* thought. I knew at this moment I needed to reach out to Human Resources. This would be the first time I'd contacted Human Resources in my ten-year banking career over a personal matter. My knuckles started turning white as I heard the clicks on the keyboard. I hit send.

Human Resources Complaint JP Morgan Chase

To whom this may concern,

Case #: XXXXXXX-X

> *On February 6th, I brought up a complaint to my manager. The previous night February 5th, 2020, I had attended a Gala thrown by JP Morgan Chase and had*

received "the 2020 Culture Advocacy Award." A night that should have been one of the happiest evenings of my life turned into the most humiliating experience of my career. When my name was announced, I walked to the front and listened to my manager speak to the attendees about why I earned the Culture Advocacy Award. During my manager's speech, a large disruption broke out; I noticed that the disturbance was coming from a few Financial Advisers, and Personal Bankers, specifically Bradley Morrison, a Partner for JP Morgan Chase. There laughs were loud enough to reach the attention of my Regional Director Jack Anderson, who actually had to shout at the audience to, "Please be quiet, and give your attention to John Wilson."

After the Awards Ceremony, one of my fellow branch managers asked if I was all right? The branch manager informed me that she believed she overheard Bradley Morrison saying sexually explicit comment about me but could not hear the exact words that he said, and at that time asked that it remain confidential. I left the event feeling violated, and humiliated. I never in my wildest dreams thought that I would experience lewd remarks directed toward me at a sober company event, during which the individual who made the comments was blatantly drunk. On February 7th, 2020 I informed my manager John Wilson that I would like a Partner change due to the lewd comments Mr. Morrison made about me that had caused the loud disruption at the Gala event. Furthermore, I informed Mr. Wilson that a traumatic event outside of work had happened with

Bradley where I felt violated, and that I did not feel comfortable or safe working with him.

During the HR investigation, I asked my manager if it were possible for Mr. Morrison to not work at my branch. My manager let me know that this would not be possible until the HR investigation concluded. I started a leave of absence on March 2nd, 2020, as it was unbearable to work in the same office space as Mr. Morrison. When my manager asked the reason for my leave of absence, I informed him it was due to the traumatic event that happened with Mr. Morrison outside of work, and also because the sexual comment lobbied at me at the Gala was one of the most humiliating experiences of my life. I informed my manager that I did not want to continue to work in an environment where I did not feel comfortable or safe. My manager informed me on March 13th, 2020 that HR had concluded their investigation and that Mr. Morrison would not be covering my branch any longer.

While I was happy to hear that I would not have to work with Mr. Morrison I was disappointed to hear that HR's investigation into Mr. Morrison's sexually harassing comments the night of the Gala was deemed inconclusive. I returned to work on April 27th, 2020, after much therapy and many doctor visits. Shortly after returning, I spoke to the manager of the HR representative responsible for conducting the investigation (and she assured me that Mr. Morrison had been reassigned from my branch.

On July 10th, 2020, I received a call from my manager, Mr. Wilson, asking if I could help manage the Main Branch as one of the employees had tested positive for COVID-19, and as a result the entire team was quarantined. I was hesitant at first but agreed to his request because I didn't want to let my manager down. However, I contacted my manager shortly after and asked if he had any other branch manager's that could cover? I let him know in this second call that I was not comfortable working at the branch and that I felt anxious and fearful of running into Mr. Morrison while covering for the branch. Mr. Wilson gave me his word that I would not see Mr. Morrison as he was on a mandatory 14-day quarantine leave. He got off the phone quickly as he said he had other issues to tend to. The conversation with Mr. Wilson felt dismissive and I do not believe he appreciated the severity of my emotions with regard to what was expressed during both phone calls.

I covered the Main Branch from July 13th-16th until Mr. Wilson was able to find a replacement for me. On July 15th, I spoke to Mr. Wilson, thanked him for finding a replacement to take over the next day, and that, "I never wanted to be placed in a situation where I felt uncomfortable, and unsafe, I told Mr. Wilson that Mr. Morrison is the only human being in the world that I did not want to be around. Seeing Mr. Morrison compromises my mental health. I wanted Mr. Wilson to understand the severity of this situation so that our conversation could be the end of it.

On July 16th, 2020, while I was completing compliance tasks with the new branch manager covering the Main Branch, Mr. Morrison came to the branch (6 days after being exposed to Covid-19). Mr. Morrison gave me a smirk and greeted me while I completed ATM tasks with the incoming branch manager. I left the bank as quickly as I could and informed my manager that Mr. Morrison was working in the Main Branch, even though I was given a verbal guarantee that he would not be there, and despite the fact that he had been placed on a mandatory 14-day quarantine as a result to exposure of COVID-19.

Prior to this experience, Mr. Wilson and I had a great work relationship. However, I felt extremely hurt that he could put me in a situation that impacted my mental health and safety. On July 20th, 2020 my manager contacted me upon the recommendation of a peer, and I let him know that being in contact with Mr. Morrison had impacted my mental health tremendously. I informed my manager that I was shocked he could put me in this situation knowing everything I had been through with this individual. Additionally, I informed my manager that my trust towards him had been negatively impacted.

On August 21st,2020 I experienced the same situation once again. While working at the North Branch location (which I had been covering for the past four months as a request from Mr. Wilson), Mr. Morrison visited the branch for an appointment. Mr. Morrison notified a

Personal Banker 15 minutes in advance by phone but did not notify management, as it is customary. I called my manager once again to report what had happened once again and asked why I hadn't been notified? When Mr. Wilson asked that I give Mr. Morrison the benefit of the doubt, and suggested that maybe Mr. Morrison didn't know that I was working at the North Branch? I informed my manager that a mutual client let me know Mr. Morrison was aware of my working location. In fact, the mutual client mentioned that Mr. Morrison had informed him of my whereabouts only a few days prior. Mr. Wilson promised that he would discuss the situation with Mr. Morrison's manager, and that it would not happen again.

On September 1st, 2020, Mr. Morrison came to the branch at 9:30 am. Once again Mr. Morrison failed to notify anyone (which is not standard protocol, (regardless of our work dispute situation). I informed my peer manager David Anderson that Mr. Morrison and I were not to be working together, and that I did not feel comfortable. I left the branch, and Mr. Anderson had a brief opportunity to speak to Mr. Morrison privately. Mr. Anderson asked Mr. Morrison if he could give him a heads up if he has an appointment at the branch so that he could make sure there is a desk available, and that while he did not know much of what was going on between Mr. Morrison and I, he would like both Mr. Morrison, and I to feel comfortable in our work environment. Mr. Morrison let Mr. Anderson know that he had notified my Manager Mr. Wilson that he had an appointment at the North Branch. I received a call from Mr. Wilson informing me that Mr. Morrison had told him that he was coming to the North Branch and that he forgot to let me know. He apologized quickly and hung-up the phone.

This situation has been beyond violating. My manager has not considered my feelings, and never provided me the appropriate tools and resources that I need to feel safe. Some of my fears about voicing my concern are I do not want to be retaliated against. Over the last few years, I have worked very hard to start the year ranked as a Performance Level 1 (Top 5% of performers in the company), and was ranked as a Performance Level 1 within the most recent scorecard that was released in August. By sharing my concern, I hope that my manager still honors my bonus as a Performance Level 1 at the end of this year. I hope that I do not get unfair treatment for voicing my concern regarding Mr. Morrison, who has been praised time and time again for his stellar performance, and the investment growth/revenue he brings to JP Morgan Chase. Yet, his behavior towards me and his inappropriate comments have gone unchecked. I hope that I will be treated with respect, care, and fairness for bringing to light an unjust situation.

I want you to know a little bit about my background. I have been a Branch Manager for JP Morgan Chase for almost five years with 10+ years in the banking industry. In all this time, I have never had a Human

Resources issue until now. I am currently the Co-Site Lead for PRIDE for Portland, OR. I have started leading a series of career development fairs to develop our Portland, OR team member's skill set to be the most valuable asset for JP Morgan Chase. I send out a Weekly Recognition email every Monday that recognizes team members who go above and beyond for each other. I participate and organize weekly calls with my manager and peers to discuss how we can continue to grow our bankers and deepen our client's relationship around Deposit & Investment Growth. I am a proud Dominican/American female, raised in a household that taught me when something is wrong YOU must use your voice so that you can be heard.

I do not want this traumatic event to define me. However, I do want to work in an environment where I feel safe, protected, and respected and know that to be possible at JP Morgan Chase. I will continue to give 110% to work each day. I will continue to be involved within my community and work with different business lines to promote diversity, inclusion, and respect. I have tried time and time again to address my concern with my manager. These attempts have been unsuccessful and personally damaging. This attempt is my last hope, and I am pleading that HR takes my concern's seriously.

My ask is that anytime there is a company-sponsored event, the company set clear expectations that sexual, racist, and or homophobic comments will not be tolerated. Doing this will ensure that all employees feel safe, respected and that they can bring their best selves to work. Attached is a photo of the humiliation that was captured while the outburst at the Gala happened. I hope that no employee feels the way I felt during a company-sponsored event where they should feel safe and respected. I ask that If a concern is brought up to HR it be taken seriously and thoroughly investigated. I had a clear understanding after speaking to HR Representative Mary that Mr. Morrison was not to cover my Branch as the Financial Adviser, nor go to my Branch for appointments. Likewise, I had a clear understanding with Mr. Wilson that Mr. Morrison would not be working in the same location as me. Both of these company representatives let me down and failed to acknowledge my mental health, and safety in the workplace. I ask that I be notified if Mr. Morrison has an appointment at whatever Branch I may be covering so that I can plan accordingly, and be outside of the Branch at that time. I would like to understand how the current policy stands with Bradley and I working together and what I can do to ensure that I feel safe at work.

I love what I do for Chase Bank, but I have been so discouraged in how this situation has been handled that I have recently told my manager that I would like to pursue another career outside of Chase. Before the Gala I could have never imagined leaving the bank or company that I loved. It is my hope that this situation can be handled with respect, care, and compassion, and

I can restore my faith in the process, and company that I have grown to respect over the last few years.

I am looking forward to hearing back from you soon.

Sincerely,
Melissa Work

A lady from Human Resources called me shortly after. "You have my word that you will not see Bradley again. He has been instructed to not go to near where you are at."

I felt relieved. There was something about her demeanor that provided me comfort.

My manager let me know that he had news to share regarding the reopening of my branch. I gathered my team members so we could hear the good news together. Things were starting to look up! I couldn't wait to be back at my home branch and see my regular clients and team members. I saw my phone ringing and clicked on the green button.

"Hello, Melissa, do you have a moment to speak?" asked John.

"I do," I responded.

"Senior leadership has decided to close most grocery store locations. Your branch will be closing in approximately three months," said John.

I was shocked. I was hit from left field and had no idea this was coming. I had to tell my team in a few minutes that our branch would forever be closed and break their hearts too. There were so many questions that flooded my mind. *Why was Chase pulling out of all grocery store locations? Would I get to say goodbye to my clients? How could I have been so naïve?*

As the weeks went by I never heard back from John regarding my request to reopen my branch temporarily to say goodbye to my clients. It was at this moment I knew I wanted to send an email to all of the employees impacted by Chase's business decision to close the grocery store locations. The way that senior leadership closed our branches was wrong and impacted hundreds of employees. I started to type a draft of what I wanted to say but had to wait until February 17, 2021, to send this email as I would get my annual bonus that I had worked so hard for. February 17, 2021, could not come soon enough.

8

LEAVING CORPORATE AMERICA AND DATING MY NEW BOYFRIEND

I was writing in a coffee shop when a man approached me. He had brown hair, blue eyes and was tall. He asked if he could sit across the table from me and I nodded my head. I didn't want to be rude, but I didn't want to be bothered.

"Where are you from?" the man asked. We made small talk. He offered to give me a snack and I politely accepted. Our hands rubbed up against one another and I pulled back. I told myself, he isn't Bradley. He wasn't even Harry, who I had dated after Bradley.

I started hanging out with Harry in November 2020. Harry is six foot, one inch with beautiful blue eyes. Harry is full of energy and brightened any room he walked into. We met at Chase Bank. Harry would create fun nicknames for the specific day of the week. "Marvelous Monday," he would say. Harry was dating another girl at the same time I was dating Quincy, so I didn't think anything of it. Harry and his girlfriend split in September 2020. Harry and I started talking and developed a friendship. I loved the friendship we were growing.

I told Harry my plans of quitting my job and my desire to travel to my mother's homeland of Dominican Republic. I couldn't believe the question I was about to ask Harry. "Would you want to join me when I go to the Dominican Republic?" I asked. My stomach started to turn. I thought he must think I'm crazy, because we were recently establishing a new friendship.

"Are you kidding me?! I would love to join you!" responded Harry. I looked into Harry's eyes. "Yes!" said Harry. Harry wrapped his arm around me, and I blushed as I looked at the floor.

A few days later Harry and I purchased our one-way tickets to arrive in the Dominican Republic on February 20, 2021. I woke up like any other morning but knew today would be much different. I was brewing with excitement and nervousness. I was making the biggest career change of my life. I was about to send an email to every employee in the state of Oregon and leave my nine-to-five corporate job.

Where's my cute, form-fitting slacks and nice top? I put them on and found my nice black heels. I used my hand to fit my right heel, then left heel. My manager had a meeting to visit my branch in the morning. I was anxious because I knew shortly after giving John my two-week notice I would be sending an email to the state of Oregon and all senior leadership—thus ending any opportunity I had at getting rehired at JP Morgan Chase Bank. 8:30 am rolled around and I saw John at the front door.

"Are you sure you want to do this, Melissa?"

Right after I send this email there is no going back! I will forever be banned from working at JP Morgan Chase Bank. I asked myself one question: *What would dad do?* I remember my dad telling me about a time that he worked at a law firm in his late twenties. My father stood up to his boss by writing a letter that highlighted the unethical practices the law firm was doing that hurt the very people they claimed to be wanting to help. At that moment I knew what I needed to do. I hit the send button.

I handed John my keys, and with that I was free. I walked out to my car. The sun was shining. I was carrying a box full of pictures, awards, and last-minute items that I wanted to bring home with me. I opened my car and knew that today would be the beginning of my new life—outside of corporate America. I was following my father's footsteps and heading to my mother's homeland of Dominican Republic to celebrate with the most handsome man in three days. Life was starting to look up.

I grabbed my phone and clicked on Harry's contact. "Are you ready for our trip?!" I asked.

I felt excitement and nervousness creeping in. This trip was going to either advance our friendship romantically or we would remain good friends. Regardless, I saw this as a win-win. I got off the plane and the warm air felt like a bath. Colors brighter than I remember. My hands were shaking so I took Harry's hand. In five minutes we would be seeing my cousin, who is like a protective brother, and I was bringing Harry, not having any idea where we stood.

My cousin was standing at the front of the home. My cousin is six foot, six inches. He has the whitest teeth and biggest smile. I opened the door and ran into his arms. It has been far too long since I've seen him. The Dominican Republic is known for fostering some of the best baseball players in the world. My cousin played major league baseball in the United States for over ten years and was now playing baseball in the Dominican Republic.

Harry and I got settled and were exhausted from the travels. Shortly after, we fell asleep and shared a king bed where we both passed out on opposite ends of the bed. The sun rose early and the light started shining bright in the room. I opened my eyes and saw that Harry was getting ready for the day. I wore my comfortable black Lululemon yoga pants and a plain white t-shirt. Harry wore brown shorts and a green shirt that brought out his eyes. He was looking as handsome as ever. We explored the monument in Santiago, Dominican Republic, and had a Presidente, which is the most popular Dominican beer. Harry took a swig as he licked his lips. Here I was in Santiago, where my parents fell in love forty-four years earlier.

My father told me it had been a blazing hot day in the Dominican Republic in September 1977. He had been wearing a white shirt with his beloved navy blue Levi jeans and had been headed to the university. He had spied the most beautiful woman he had ever laid eyes on. She had medium brown hair that shaped her face perfectly and big puppy like brown eyes. She had been standing on the corner with another woman. He had pulled up in his beaten-up blue Volkswagen and yelled, "Senoritas, do you need a ride to the University?"

They said, "Si."

He had asked what their names were and when my mom introduced herself he had felt butterflies. My mother had started to approach his vehicle and he had been thunderstruck. Her hair had blown in the wind and her eyes met his. He had a feeling deep in his stomach that he had never experienced before. As he was driving to the university he couldn't help but glance in the rearview mirror.

My mother had an innocence and beauty about her which was unlike any he had ever seen. The way she glazed out the window looked picturesque. He had known subconsciously that she was the one. My mother got out of the car with her sister and started walking to class. He had sat in the car and he couldn't help but think, "Do not let her get away." He had known at this moment that he needed to muster the courage to ask for her phone number.

He pulled his car onto the side street as fast as he could and started to run in the direction she took off. He was out of breath when he reached my mom. "Senorita!" he yelled.

My mom turned around and looked surprised.

"Senorita, I would be a fool if I didn't ask. Can I please have your phone number?" he said.

"I can give you my number under one condition," she responded.

He said he had been panting and tried to compose himself by keeping his hands on his knees. "What's that?" he asked.

"That we are just friends," she responded.

He was grateful that he was able to secure her phone number to start working his magic.

My mother was born in Santiago, Dominican Republic, and came from a family of thirteen children. She had six brothers and six sisters. When the sun started to climb she would rise with it. The birds would sing and the chickens would speak. This was my mother's favorite part of the day. If you experienced a day in her life, it was complete chaos. Having thirteen children in one household is no easy task. When my mother went to school it was her safe place. She had loved to read and treasured every moment of silence.

The moment my father laid eyes on my mother he had known he was in it for the long haul. The first obstacle was asking for my mother's number and the second obstacle was asking permission from my grandfather to date his daughter. The culture in the Dominican Republic was much different than that in the United States. Before you start dating a girl you need to ask for her father's permission.

My mother had just finished her school day. She was wearing a long red skirt, a loose white shirt and a headband that wrapped her black wavy hair perfectly. She had gotten out of his car and my father had taken a deep breath. This would be the first time he approached my mother's front door. He had worn his finest clothes and tripped over his feet as he landed at the door. My mother's father answered on his second knock.

"Hello!" said my grandfather. My father bit his tongue and couldn't get a word out. "How can I help you?" asked my grandfather.

"Well sir, I have a question to ask," my father said. "I was hoping I could date your daughter?"

"Which one?" asked my grandfather.

"Gloria," my father responded.

My grandfather slammed the door in my father's face. My father left the home with his shoulders sinking low and walked as quickly as he could to his car. He had opened the front door and sat inside. As the months went on he was persistent. He had mustered the courage to speak to my grandfather and after his third try my grandfather said that he could date Gloria if they hung out at his home under his or her brother's supervision.

The day my mother met my father was one of the most memorable days of her life. She had dated my father for a year before they kissed. It's really quite a funny story about how their first kiss happened. She said that they'd play chess every evening. One evening my father gathered the courage to ask my mother for a kiss if he beat her.

"Senorita, if I beat you in chess, can I have a kiss?" he asked.

"You may, but do you think you're going to win?" she responded.

They played chess, and guess what? My mother won! Had she wanted to win? No. She'd wanted my dad to win so that he would finally kiss her, but she wasn't ready to be defeated that easily.

 "There's always next time," he said.

My mother looked into my father's eyes. "I'm ready for my kiss," she said.

"But I lost!" said my father.

"If you don't kiss me tonight, then I won't give you the chance again."

My father ran his hand through her hair and kissed my mother gently. She felt butterflies instantly—it was at this moment she had known she was falling in love with her American blue-eyed man named James Richard Work.

My father continued to visit my mother's home five days a week and got to know her family. It was 7 pm when my mother's brothers went to their rooms and my mom and dad started speaking in the living room.

"Finally we get some alone time," said my father.

My mother was wearing a long white dress that had small blue flowers. It cupped her body perfectly and she looked like an angel when she smiled.

"You look so beautiful right now," said my father.

My mother started to blush and he saw a smile appearing from her lips. He heard a small noise and turned around. Under the long white curtains he saw two feet. *Oh my god is someone behind the curtains?* My father knew those shoes too well. My grandfather was hiding behind the curtains.

"It's getting late. I better get home," he said. He gave my mother a hug and went to his car. "Thank goodness I didn't talk about our kiss in front of her dad," he later said.

After their first kiss he had known he wanted to propose, all in due time. He asked my mom to be his wife in early 1980. My mother said yes and moved to the United States with him. He had always said that being with my mom was magical. He had met his pea in a pod. My parents would do amber shows together, travel to new places, and go on hikes around Oregon. They had three beautiful children. Two boys and one girl, and that is when I had come along.

I was falling for Harry like my father had fallen in love with my mother in the Dominican Republic. The next week Harry and I were off to Puerta Plata. We would be spending the rest of our time there, and I was excited for what was to come. We arrived in Puerto Plata on March 1, 2021, and it was like a scene out of the movies. The water was glistening. The resort was beautiful and the pools were peaceful. The palm trees surrounded us, and everything was fresh and green. We stayed in a small studio on the beach, and the environment couldn't have been more romantic.

A few of my friends thought that Harry liked me. Call me silly, but I thought we were just getting to be good friends, and at this point we had kissed once, so I wasn't sure if we would make it out of the friend zone.

"Do you want to get some food?" asked Harry.

"Yes!" I responded.

As we walked to the restaurant, I saw a blue bench. "There's something I've been meaning to ask you," said Harry.

We stopped at the bench and sat. I started tapping my foot on the ground. *What in the world does he want to talk to me about?* I thought. When I looked at Harry I saw that he was rubbing his pant legs and looking straight at the ground.

His voice started trembling. "I've been meaning to ask you. What do you think of me? Of us?" asked Harry.

My stomach started turning and I was trying to meet Harry's eyes but he continued to stare at the ground. "You're an amazing man! What do you mean about us?" I asked.

Harry continued to rub his legs and I saw a droplet of sweat fall to the ground. He rubbed his forehead with his palm. "I think you know I like you," said Harry.

I felt butterflies deep inside my stomach and a jolt of electricity run through my upper chest. "Well… I kind of thought you might have a crush on me," I said.

Harry stopped rubbing his legs, sat up straight, and turned his face toward me. "Melissa, I would like you to be my girlfriend."

A million thoughts started racing through my mind. Of course I adore Harry, but getting into a committed relationship was a decision I did not take lightly.

"Can I think about it for a bit?" I asked.

We had a pleasant dinner, but then reality hit. Harry just asked me to be his girlfriend! I wanted to say yes, but Harry had recently moved to Boise, Idaho, which was a six-hour drive from Portland. I don't know how I felt about doing long distance. I thought long and hard and came up with my decision the next day.

Harry was folding his clothes and dancing to the music that was playing on his stereo. I grabbed Harry's arm gently and looked into his eyes. The words flowed out of my mouth like a river.

"I thought about what you asked, and yes I would like to be your girlfriend!" I said.

Harry couldn't contain the smile on his face, and his eyes glistened more than I had noticed in the past. When Harry and I made it official, I texted Quincy the next day. I wanted Quincy to hear from me that I had started a new relationship. I'll never forget the moment I got the courage to finally send it. My hands were poised over the keys and my eyes were watering. I was in a parallel universe of falling in love with a new man and not knowing how to let go of my first true love.

Just like that I was in a new long-distance relationship. I was falling in love with the kindest and most handsome man. Harry and I would speak nonstop every day, and he wished me a good night each evening. I would have moments where I thought: *Where did I find this guy?!* Harry and I discussed our future goals, our dreams, and having a family of our own one day and what that would look like. We seemed to agree on everything and I remember thinking that I finally found my perfect match. But still, I was letting Quincy go.

9

ALFACAR, SPAIN

On my journey, I was letting other things go. I stopped wearing makeup. I stopped caring about what people thought about me. I stopped checking my phone constantly and I started to feel free. Lily and I decided that today was going to be full of nature. Lily found a viewing area that was supposed to be beautiful. I found a breakfast place called Marley Casual Bar in Alfacar, Spain, that looked nice.

There was a ginormous painting of a beautiful black woman with red lips and white teeth that captivated my view.

"Can I have a cappuccino and an avocado tostada?" I asked. I was falling in love with Spanish food. I always ate three-course meals in the states, but here I grazed, and it felt better. After breakfast we got gas at a local gas station and needed to fill the air in Lilly's tires. It was my first time filling tires with air. I hoped I was doing this right. We set the air meter to what the vehicle said, and it was much easier than I expected. I stood up straight and walked to the next tire.

I got into the car and it felt much more elevated. I hadn't realized how low the air in the tires had been. The sunroof was off and we were enjoying the fresh wind hitting our faces. We were blasting music in the car as I put my arms up in a V position and felt the air move through my hair. My dad and I loved to play Eminem and Karen Carpenter on the ride to school. Both artists differed tremendously, but we loved them just the same. My dad and I would sing in unison.

My dad was driving his bright blue Ford, and the stereo was rocking with our bodies dancing along. He learned every word Eminem would rap in his songs and I learned every word Karen Carpenter would sing. I had sung to "Lose Yourself" and was shocked when my dad started rapping with me. He must have played this song on repeat like I had to remember all the words. We rapped "Lose Yourself" in unison. The next moment my dad said, "Let's switch the CD to Karen Carpenter." My dad played "Mr. Postman" by the Carpenters. I was an eighth grader singing a song that was released in 1975 and having the time of my life.

Lily and I made it to the top of the mountain and could now take in one of the most beautiful views of my life. The sun was shining on the Sierra Nevada Mountains. Sierra Nevada means "Snowy mountains," and it was just that. I started to feel stronger. I sat cress cross with my face held up to the sky. My posture was starting to change from the downward slump to tall and straight.

We decided to check out one more view point. The location was called Huetor de Santillan and was ironically only 6 minutes away from our hotel. I continued to sip on wine and at this point felt a little tipsy. The red wine tasted so good on my lips.

"What motivated you to work as a branch manager at a bank so young?" asked Lily.

In the spring of 2009 I had known that it was time to apply to colleges. I sent an application to the University of Oregon and got accepted. I was officially going to be a Duck. I would move into my own apartment and start living the life of an official adult! There was only one problem: I needed to get a job.

In October 2010 I applied for over twenty jobs with no luck. I called my dad. "No one wants to hire me. You are going to have to support me until I'm forty at the rate I'm going."

My father chuckled. "Keep applying to jobs, honey. One manager will see your potential."

"Why haven't the last twenty?" I asked. Here I was a sophomore at the University of Oregon-relying on my dad to pay for my food, clothes, rent, and any activity I did with my friends. I felt like a loser. The end of the month was my least favorite because I knew I needed to start calling my dad to beg for rent money.

When my dad heard the word "rent," he'd hang up, and like clockwork I'd call him back and plead for rent money. Each month my strategy would change. I would wait until the middle of the conversation before I asked for rent money or ask my dad about his day. No matter what excuse I threw at my dad, his response never changed. He would hang up and by the third of the month he would transfer just enough money for me to get by. After the third month I was determined to get a job.

My father pitched the idea about me working for a bank. I visited two local branches and really liked the idea of it. I'd heard there were great benefits and that I would get paid on holidays. What could be better than that?! Two weeks later, I had a job at a bank. The first call I made was to tell my dad the great news. After I passed a background check I started working at Wells Fargo Bank. I wanted to succeed so that I didn't have to call my dad to beg for money. I excelled quickly and became the youngest branch manager in the state of Oregon by age twenty-two.

Reflecting back on my father's tactic—it motivated me to work hard. I worked for Wells Fargo for five years until I got recruited to JP Morgan Chase. I worked in the banking industry altogether for ten years," I told Lily.

When we got back to the hotel I enjoyed a nice hot shower and got into some comfortable clothes. I called my parents to check in with them. "I am going to journal!" said Lily. This gave me the idea to write my story. I sat down and drew out some paper, when I started writing I couldn't drop my pen. There was so much that had happened over the last few years. As I started to write I faced the trauma, and the reality of what had happened. It was as if the pen had a life of its own and it was ready to free me from the pain I had held on for far too long. This trip had unleashed the sorrow and now, with writing, I could help heal it: my breakups, my rape, and of course, the troubles with my father.

10

ONE WAY TICKET TO THE MAYO CLINIC

July, 2021

I couldn't get the comment Judge Boris said out of my mind. What did she mean by anesthesiologist's record? I saw a web page where you could insert someone's name and then it shows their medical record.

http://omb.oregon.gov/search

I typed "Ashley Alkinson" and saw that she had a medical malpractice case.

Malpractice Claims

> **Reported:**
> 10/21/2015
> Location: Medford, OR
>
> **Disposition:**
> (1) Settled by parties

Date Closed:
02/06/2017

Total Indemnity Insurer Paid on behalf of defendant:
$1,000,000

Allegation:
High risk anesthesia patient coded shortly following anesthesia induction.

This prompted me to look over all of the anesthesiologists' records in the Rogue Valley and I found that Ashley Alkinson was the only anesthesiologist that had a medical malpractice lawsuit/citation on her record. I was astonished to find out that Ashley Alkinson had a $1,000,000 lawsuit on her record and that the defense's main argument was that my father should have never had surgery. Unbeknownst to me, one of Chad Cunningham's peers in Medford said, "Your father was too high functioning to receive this surgery."

If I had known this information earlier, I would have pursued a lawsuit against Chad Cunningham for recommending an unnecessary surgery. That Ashley Alkinson had an egregious citation in her record was astonishing. One of my father's favorite sayings was "Birds of a feather flock together." My father taught me to follow my instincts. After three years I found out that this surgery should have never happened in the first place.

I asked myself, *Why would Dr. Cunningham complete an unnecessary invasive surgery?* I realized it all boiled down to money. Doctors are often incentivized to perform surgery. It was no surprise that I found out Dr. Cunningham completes the most surgeries out of any of his fellow peers in Medford. I had to tell my brother. In the meantime, my father started getting worse.

I needed to take my father to the world-renowned Mayo Clinic, and by July 14, 2021, my father and I were off on two one-way tickets to Rochester, Minnesota. When I picked up my father, he looked frail, weighed 138 pounds, and could barely walk. My heart broke but I equally had perseverance that I needed to give it my all and get my father to the Mayo Clinic.

"Dad, I know that you can't speak to me right now. I know this may be confusing but I am going to be with you every step of the way. I am taking you to the Mayo Clinic to find doctors that can help you. I promise I will not leave your side," I said.

My father looked at me with what little energy he had left and smiled. I saw a small nod and knew that I had his blessing. I'll never forget my connecting flight going to Rochester, MN. An older woman sitting beside me introduced herself as a retired doctor who had previously worked at the Mayo Clinic. She glanced at my father and her eyes widened as she grabbed my arm to give me a gentle squeeze. "I sure hope you are taking your father to the Mayo Clinic," she said.

I looked at her and let her know I was.

"How long have you been on the waiting list? Six months? Seven?" asked the retired doctor.

"A little over six months," I responded.

At this point I realized how crazy I would sound if I told her that I wasn't on a waiting list and that my plan was to go into the emergency room praying that my father would be admitted. I got an Airbnb for my father and me to allow us to rest for one day and the next day my plan went into full motion. "Melissa, you are a good daughter," my father said slowly as he stared at the floor. Before that sentence my father hadn't spoken more than ten words over the last few months. It reassured me that I was doing the right thing, and no matter what the outcome was I was giving it my all to try to save my father's life.

On July 18, 2021, I took my dad to the emergency room and sat next to him, waiting to be seen. Two hours went by rather quickly. After the third hour, a man yelled, "Good luck being seen at the Mayo Clinic! It's harder to be seen here than getting into Harvard." He proceeded to walk out the door.

What in the world was I thinking of, bringing my father across the country? I thought to myself. The clock kept ticking, and after five hours an admissions representative announced, "James Work, they are ready to see you." I took a deep breath and wheeled my father to the small office.

"What brings you to the Mayo Clinic?" asked the doctor.

I explained my father's surgery, how he was unable to eat for six months and was placed on a feeding tube. How my father started to get better where he could eat and walk but started declining to where he is at now. "My hope in bringing my father to the Mayo Clinic is that we get a concrete diagnosis in hopes that my father can have a full recovery," I said.

At this point I didn't want to tell the doctor about my father's catatonia diagnosis in case my father had received the wrong diagnosis at OHSU. The doctor looked at me with sincerity in her eyes, "I can't imagine what you've been through. I know you have traveled far. Unfortunately, the medical system is broken and it is very hard to admit someone through inpatient care. The soonest we could have your father seen is in four months, outpatient," said the doctor.

My stomach sank. It was time I do whatever I could to try to get my father admitted. "My father was diagnosed with catatonia a few months after his surgery at OHSU. I wonder if he could have fallen into that same state now?" I said.

The doctor scratched her head as she looked at my father. "I'll bring a psychiatrist and see what his thoughts are. If your father has fallen into a catatonic state, then we will admit him," said the doctor.

I felt like I was about to crumble as I waited anxiously for the psychiatrist to walk through the door. His eyes met mine, and then he moved his face toward my father. "We can try the Ativan challenge to treat your father's catatonic state. If the Ativan challenge doesn't work, your father will spend the night in the hospital and can leave in the morning. We can then look at outpatient care. If the Ativan challenge works, I will talk to you about next steps," said the psychiatrist.

"What is the Ativan challenge?" I asked.

"The Ativan challenge uses two milligrams of lorazepam through an IV to determine the likelihood of a catatonia diagnosis," said the psychiatrist.

After waiting fifteen minutes (what seemed like an eternity) the doctor came back and asked if some of his colleagues could observe my father during the Ativan challenge.

"Yes, that is okay," I said.

"Is it okay if we video record your father?" asked the doctor.

I nodded my head. Here I was in Rochester, Minnesota with eight doctors gathered around, exhausted and praying that my father would be admitted.

"I am ready to administer Ativan. Is it okay, Doctor?" asked the nurse.

"Yes, go ahead," responded the doctor.

A few minutes after the nurse administered Ativan, it was like a light went on in my father's mind. My father moved his arms up and stretched, then looked at me with concerned eyes.

"What are we doing in Minnesota, and why are we at the Mayo Clinic?" asked my father.

The doctor's mouth opened wide. I fell to my knees. The medication that was given to my father worked and in turn granted him acceptance into the Mayo Clinic. It was a miracle, one we needed to live another day. "We are admitting your father Melissa! We are going to get him ECT!" said the psychiatrist.

ECT is short for electroconvulsive therapy and is a treatment that has been extremely effective for people who have suffered from catatonia and or severe depression. It can be a game changer and has an effectiveness rate of 85%. ECT has evolved tremendously and is one of the most effective methods to treat severe depression and, in my father's case, catatonia, said the psychiatrist. I stayed on my knees as I heard a cry come from my mouth. I have never felt as emotional in my life. I lifted my arms and yelled, "Thank you, Lord," as I rested my head on the floor.

The psychiatrist squeezed my shoulder. "Melissa, we are going to get your father better."

I lifted my head and looked up toward the psychiatrist and started to feel a glimmer of hope.

"We cannot answer why there was such a stark difference after your father's operation or how he developed catatonia, but ECT has definitely helped your father improve," said the psychiatrist.

By August 26, 2021, my father had started speaking and sounding more like himself. He had gained twenty pounds and was starting to do physical activity.

I heard a ding on my phone and saw that I received an email from Mr. Wilson:

> *We're eager to hear how the Mayo Clinic trip went and how your dad is doing. After initial good indications, has his condition improved? Any news will be appreciated.*

My fingers started moving quickly on my keyboard and I responded,

> *On August 26th, 2021 my father started speaking and sounding much more like himself. He has gained 20 pounds and is starting to do more physical activity. I spoke to my father on August 27th 2021 regarding the lawsuit and the result. My father was coherent and asked many questions. He wanted me to thank you and Mrs. Newberg for the remarkable job that you did and*

the difference you both have made within our family's life. Fast forward to today my father has consistently walked one mile each day (4 laps on the local track). He is gradually gaining weight and has been smiling much more as well as engaging in conversation.

I was starting to get my person back—my father. Losing my father was the worst thing that ever happened to me but getting him back was equally the best. I could travel back home to Portland and get back to my normal routine of seeing my friends and, most important, Harry. I was sitting in my apartment packing last-minute items I heard a ding and looked at my phone. I'd received a message on Instagram from a girl named Caleigh. I had to accept it because we didn't have any mutual friends, and I saw that it was long.

As I opened the message I got a sick feeling in my stomach, and then I took in the words:

> "Hey girl I'm really so incredibly sorry to have to tell you this but I live in Boise, Idaho and I matched with Harry on tinder about two months ago. We hung out multiple times, I slept over at his place and everything like that and he even bought me a gift, and when he was traveling to Minnesota he told me he was with family and he was with you, when he came back from Minnesota I told him I wasn't seeing anyone else and he told me he wasn't either, I had absolutely no idea that he had a girlfriend he actually blocked me from all of his social media and I found out when I looked him up to tell my friends about him, and that's when I found out about you. You seem like a really sweet

girl and he told me that he told you about us but I don't really feel like he did so if he did tell you already I apologize but he lied to me and when I found out about you I confronted him. He told me he had been wanting to break up with you for a while and just didn't know how to tell you. Here is one of the photos he sent me. If you would like to see the rest I can show you but they are more explicit, if you want to talk at all please feel free to reach out to me as well. Again I am so incredibly sorry. –Caleigh."

I called Caleigh.

"I am so sorry to be the bearer of bad news," said Caleigh.

"It's not that I don't believe you, but could you send me your text messages?" I asked.

Caleigh sent me a copy of their text messages, and I knew that everything she told me was true. I felt helpless. How did the man I fall in love with do this to me? How could my judge of character be so off? In an instant my life had been turned upside down.

I had dated some real losers in the past but this was different. My friends adored Harry, my best friends thought he was my perfect match, and my father recently met Harry when he'd accompanied me at the Mayo Clinic the week prior. My sadness turned into anger. How could Harry do this to me? Especially at my lowest point? I managed to type Harry's phone number.

"Hello, honey!" said Harry. When he heard my voice he knew that something was wrong.

"Caleigh messaged me," I said. I started crying on the phone. I was hysterical. "How could you?!" I asked.

Surprisingly Harry took responsibility. He apologized and said that he didn't know what came over him. "The distance had grown to be an issue and I didn't know how to tell you with how much you were already going through with your dad."

As bad as I wanted to turn back the clock and wish that Caleigh hadn't messaged me, I knew that what we had was lost forever. That same day I texted Harry's sister. Under normal circumstances I wouldn't have texted her, but something in my heart inclined me to write to her. This felt so out of character for Harry. The next few weeks were a blur. I told all of my friends and family what happened. They were just as shocked as I was. For the second time in my life everyone had fallen in love with the same guy as I had. No one saw this coming, especially me.

I spoke to Harry on several occasions after, but it was never the same. As much as I wanted to hold onto the idea of Harry we both knew it was time to move forward. I never gave up hope on love. I went on dating apps, and then I met this guy named Max. When we met up for the first time, he got up after a short time and I saw him at the bar closing out his tab. The bartender handed Max his card. I thought, *He obviously isn't feeling this date, either.* Max turned around and proceeded to walk straight out the front door.

Is this seriously happening? Is my date really walking out without saying a word?

I got whatever pride I had left, walked to the bar, and asked to close out for the Moscow Mule. The shots were still at the table and I let the man to my right know that he and his friend were welcome to them. I walked outside where the droplets looked like miniature soccer balls and ran to my car.

My phone buzzed, and I saw a text from Max: "Sorry, I wasn't feeling it, and was honestly not feeling my best, either."

I got in my car and instantly deleted his phone number. I then deleted him from my Facebook and Instagram. I started to drive home as a million thoughts ambushed my mind. *What was wrong with my life?* I came home and deleted my dating app. *Never again,* I told myself.

11

GRANADA, SPAIN

January 30, 2022

The next day as I was walking to the Hammad salon I saw people dancing on the street. I stopped to observe for a few minutes. There was an older woman in a yellow dress—she looked like she was having the time of her life. There was a younger girl dancing with her mom. She was laughing and had quite the dancing skills. At the end of the song everyone started clapping. I felt so much energy. I started dancing. Never in my life did I think I would dance by myself but here I was swirling freely without one worry in the world. Turning circles and smiling to myself. I felt free.

I went to the Arabian baths. It had intricate detail at every angle you look. I dipped my toe in the warm bath and started walking inside quickly. I swam to the next side feeling a deep relief from my body. There were four large baths that were Arabian style. One was cold, one was Lukewarm, one was warm and the last was hot. There was a sauna to top it off and a place to drink hot tea. I felt so relaxed, so at peace. Where has this been my whole life? Baths are my favorite thing in the world—and now I got to enjoy four of them. I relaxed in each bath an equal amount of time except for the cold bath. I jumped in and out almost just as quickly. I heard that the cold bath is very healthy for you, but being cold was difficult for me.

After the baths I went into the sauna. I spent ten minutes in the sauna and then decided to shower. After I showered I opened my locker. My bag was gone. I searched through my locker and still couldn't find my bag. I grabbed my swimsuit, sweater, socks, and shoes and threw them back in the locker. My bag had my passport, my Covid recovery certificate, all of my credit cards, my driver's license, my air pods, my cell phone and 600 dollars.

I saw a lady next to me who was watching me. I opened my arms toward her. "Hello did you see a colorful fanny pack?" I asked.

She shook her head no. One of my worst nightmares came to reality. I can't believe I'd left my passport in that bag. I was about to have a breakdown. There's no way that someone would have returned it. After all, I'd heard that there was a tremendous amount of theft in Barcelona, and Grenada couldn't be much different.

I ran over to an employee. I pointed toward my stomach as my hands were shaking. "I have a fanny pack that is colorful and wraps around my stomach."

He held one finger up. *Wait.* I had to wait. He walked up the stairs and disappeared in the hallway. I wondered where he was going. I went into my locker one more time and then felt a tap on my shoulder. I turned around and saw that he was holding my bag up! I used my right finger to unzip my bag and saw that everything was there. This was the first time I didn't give up and realized the strength that lay in my bones.

Lily and I were off to Tarifa, Spain. I heard a song that reminded me of my father, which was "I Won't Give Up," by Jason Mraz. "After work I would drive to Providence Hospital and sing my dad this song every night," I said.

"How long was your father at Providence?" asked Lily.

"Over a month and a half. My father loved hearing my voice even though I'm not a good singer by any means," I said. I started to chuckle. "I would sing this song to him for hours on end. The words provided me comfort and kept me moving forward," I said.

As the song continued to play, Lily started singing the words. I realized the power of music and how it touches us in all different ways around the world. "Could you please play it again?" I asked. I gazed out the window.

My mother recorded me singing for my father so she could play it to him during the day when I was at work. My father would give me a small smile. This smile gave me the strength I needed to fight for my father.

One day I was visiting my father and started fudging the truth about how he was doing physically. He stared at me, and I knew he meant: *Tell me the truth.* This reminded me of a memory from high school.

Speech and debate was my world. I specialized in the Lincoln-Douglas debate. My father was on the speech and debate team throughout high school, too, and I would consult with him before

I attended any tournaments. Once, I had a big math test in the third period. I was unprepared for this test but needed to get a B in order to attend my Speech and Debate tournament. I only needed three more days to study, then I knew I would easily pass the test. I decided to forge my parents' signatures so I could postpone my test. I'll be the first to admit that I didn't have the best cursive, and reflecting back on this decision: it wasn't my wisest choice. The principal's assistant called my dad.

Then my dad called me. "Where are you, Melissa?" asked my father.

"School," I responded.

"Don't lie to me," said my father.

"How did you know I was lying?" I asked.

"Come home right now," said my father.

I started to drive home. *How had Dad known I was lying? I'm going to be in so much trouble.*

I pulled up my driveway and sat in my car for a few minutes. I walked to the front door, which was already open.

My father shrugged his shoulders as he looked down. "I'm very disappointed in you, Melissa," said my father. "Tell me the truth."

My voice started shaking and I couldn't make eye contact. "I had a math test during third period and I needed to get a B to attend the next debate tournament. I wasn't prepared for the test so I forged a note so that I could study this weekend and be more prepared for the test. I'm sorry for lying to you, but I really needed more time," I said.

My father shrugged his shoulders. "Did I raise my daughter to think that lying is okay?"

"Melissa, I want you to understand your character and integrity is all you have. Not only did you lie, you compromised your character. Nothing is worth losing your character over," said my father.

"I'm sorry, Dad, but—"

"No buts. The school called me and asked if I had signed a note excusing you to go home," said my father.

"What did you say?!" I asked.

"The truth," said my father.

My heart was jumping. I felt desperate.

"Thanks, Dad. Now I'm going to flunk my class! I don't think the teacher will even let me take the test, and I won't be able to attend the speech and debate tournament," I said.

 "Then this tournament was not meant to be. You'll learn through life you'll have spur-of-the-moment decisions to make, and the one thing I hope to teach you is to be honest—no matter how difficult your truth may be," said my father. My father put his hand out and said, "Keys."

I reluctantly hand them to him.

"I would like you to apologize to your math and speech and debate coach first thing next week, and then we can talk."

Now, Lily pulled up to Tarifa and we got situated in our hotel. It had a Moroccan theme to it—and this was much different than the other hotels I had stayed at in Spain. "How far is Morocco from Tarifa?" I asked.

"It's only a thirty-minute boat ride!" said Lily. Lily wanted to take a nap after getting food and I wanted to explore the town. I walked to the beach and fell upon the Waikiki restaurant. The music was blasting, the people were laughing and the setting was vibrant. There was a big brown couch that I made myself at home. The sun was beaming to the beat of the music. It appeared that everyone owned a dog and I saw the cutest mom dancing with her baby as they were walking out of the restaurant.

It was February 5, 2022—Lily's brother's one-year anniversary of committing suicide. I knew that it would be a heavy day. When Lily and I woke up, Lily called her mom. Once Lily got off the phone she told me that the conversation was kept light because she wanted to keep her mom happy. She told her mom about the funny story that happened with the British man and that she would call her father later. After the phone call Lily and I started getting ready for the day. I told Lily that today was my treat. When Lily and I got pizza we started talking about when her brother passed.

"One of my friends lost her grandmother the same week I lost my brother. My friend was so sad. She felt bad that she was sad about her grandmother when I had just lost my brother. I told my friend not to feel sorry that death shouldn't be about comparing losses—death is hard no matter who it is," said Lily.

There was a reason I was supposed to cross paths with Lily, and the reason was becoming clear. Lily and I walked to the Waikiki bar to have a Moscow Mule. I have never had as fruity of a Moscow

Mule before. Each sip felt so good hitting my lips.

"How are you feeling about your boy life?" asked Lily.

"I've never been at such peace before. I have no one to text or call. If we decided to take a few shots tonight I still wouldn't drunk call anyone and that feels so refreshing! It feels freeing. From time to time I think of Quincy but outside of that I feel great," I said.

While I was sitting in the sun with Lily I felt happy. My priority wasn't a man. My priority was my happiness and healing my soul. On February 13, 2022, Lily and I were off on our drive from Portugal all the way to France. It was a long drive—twenty-four hours to be exact with skipping tolls. The tolls were expensive, and Lily and I were trying to budget so that we could extend our travels for as long as possible. Lily's car is manual, and she was getting tired of doing all the driving.

"You ready to learn manual?" asked Lily.

I started rubbing my pant legs. "I'm honestly pretty scared," I said.

"Come on! You can do it!" said Lily.

"I don't know if I can. I'm thirty-one and have never driven a manual. What if I get into an accident?" I said.

"If I keep driving the whole way, then I'll get in an accident!" said Lily.

"True. Okay, I'll learn," I said.

Lily pulled over to a parking lot and we switched spots.

"You're going to have to tell me everything to do! I have absolutely no idea!" I said.

"Don't worry, I will. I'm going to switch the gears and tell you when to press the pedal and brake," said Lily.

"That sounds sketchy—but okay," I said.

"Don't worry! We can do this!" said Lily.

"All right. I'm ready," I said. I grabbed the wheel, holding on tight, my fingers turned white.

"Press the pedal and the brake," said Lily.

"Like this?"

"No, press the pedal harder," said Lily.

"Okay. I'm pressing it as hard as I can!" I said.

"Okay, now release the brake and press the gas. I'm going into the second gear," said Lily.

"Damnit, the car just turned off," I said.

"No worries! Press the brake and gas pedal at the same time and we'll turn the car back on," said Lily.

I did just this and the car turned on. Lily instructed me again and this time I got it. Lily worked the stick and I followed her instruction and we made it on the highway.

"We freaking did it!" I said.

"You did it!" said Lily.

I made a real dent in our driving. I drove three hours until Lily and I had to use the bathroom. Lily instructed me to slow down. The car stopped and the woman looking at us from the rest area started laughing out loud. In this moment I could tell she knew I was learning how to drive manual and I started laughing, too.

I found a place for 23 euros in Paterna, Spain. It looked like it was a room in a shared home, but for 23 euros I was down—Lily was too! We made it to Paterna by 9:30 pm, and the owner was waiting for us outside. We went up the elevator with him. He was the cutest old man and made us feel at home. The room was basic but cute. I snuggled up in bed as soon as I could.

"I need to use the bathroom and am honestly too tired to put my pants on," said Lily.

"Don't worry. I think the old man is sleeping," I said.

Lily tied on a sweater which barely covered her buns and rushed over to the bathroom and got back quickly.

"Was he out there?" I asked.

"No. Thank goodness.

The old cute man met us in the morning and asked how our sleep was.

And with that Lily and I were off on our quest to the French Alps!

12

CONTINUED MISTAKES

I went through a whirlwind of emotions after my breakup with Harry. The only thing I could think about was Bradley and everything that had happened between us over the past few years. I wanted to gain my power back and felt that the only way this was possible was facing my biggest fear and seeing Bradley in person. It had been a little over one year and six months since the gala happened and almost one year since I saw him last. I reached out to Bradley.

It was November 6, 2021, and I had just returned from a trip to the Dominican Republic with two of my best friends. I told all of the closest people in my life my recent encounter with Bradley the past month, and all of them had the same response: "We're worried about you Mel."

"I'll be fine. I'm capable of making my own decisions," I'd responded.

Bradley was the first person I texted when I got back to the United States, and I wanted to see him again.

We made plans to see each other one evening, and he was the only thing I could think about. I took off to meet Bradley at Victoria's again. As I parked my vehicle I felt more nervous than ever. My lips started trembling. *Stop that, Mel. You are in control.* I swung my legs out of the car and walked confidently to the bar.

What the fuck are you doing right now? I thought to myself. A part of me wanted Bradley. The other part of me thought about all the pain and the suffering Bradley put me through over the last two years. Bradley was looking down at our drinks as he made his way back and sat across from me. I couldn't stop the next words from coming out of my mouth.

"Do you feel bad?" I asked as I stared intently in his eyes.

"For what?" asked Bradley.

"For the gala and everything you put me through," I said as my lips trembled.

Bradley looked at me, and his face looked different this time. "We can talk about it when we get back to my place," he said.

I put it to rest for a moment and enjoyed my drink. "Can I have another one?" I asked.

"Yeah I'll go grab one from the bar," said Bradley.

I called my middle brother. "You won't believe who I'm with," I said.

"Who?"

"Bradley," I said.

"What the fuck are you doing?"

"I need closure."

"Call me when you get home," said my brother.

Bradley started to stumble and handed me my drink.

"Thank you." I started chugging my drink.

"Slow down there, champ," said Bradley.

"Are you ready to go back to your place?" I asked.

"You don't want another drink?" asked Bradley.

"No, I want to talk."

Bradley and I walked up the stairs. His dog ran up to the door and was wagging her tail relentlessly. I took a deep breath and sat down on his couch.

"Can I be honest?" I asked.

"What's on your mind, Melissa?" asked Bradley. His eyes look tired. He was sitting a few feet away from me and I could tell he was curious what my question would be.

"I think you're fucked up," I said.

Bradley chuckled. "Why is that?" he asked.

"You know why, Bradley. You are fucked up, and you fucked me up in the process."

"You left your career because of me." He chuckled.

Oh no, I was not going to give him this power, I thought. "I used to love what I did, and yes I left, but I did not leave because of you." I looked straight into his eyes. "Corporate America wasn't for me. Being told what to do from nine to five didn't make me happy anymore. I can find myself and be free now," I said.

Bradley swigged a White Claw as he responded. "Well, you can thank me for that," he said coldly. "Here you are mad at me and you should be thanking me." He chuckled.

"You were a part of the reason I left, but you were not the main reason," I said. I held my composure the best I could. "Why did you yell sexually explicit comments about me at the gala?" My voice sounded like it was pleading. As if an answer that Bradley gave me would remove the pain I experienced. As if anything he had to say would take away the panic attacks and endless tears that I had gone through over the last two years.

"Look, Mel, I do feel bad about that. I was fucked up at the gala," he said. "Which manager told you? It was Jason wasn't it?" Bradley asked.

"I'm not going to tell you which manager told me. The bigger reason is why the fuck did you do that?!" I yelled. My voice started rising as my throat choked. *Control yourself, Mel. Do not give him any more power.*

"I'm sorry about that, but you did get Human Resources involved. You brought the whole ordeal on yourself," he replied.

"I couldn't work with you anymore! I did whatever I could to protect you, and for what?!" I yelled. *Hold yourself together, Melissa.*

Bradley was looking at me diligently as the next words flowed out of his mouth. "Harry wouldn't even look at me when I went into work," he said.

Now I was looking at Bradley waiting for what he was about to say next. "I know what you told him. You think I fucking raped you in September," he said.

"You know how I feel about it, Bradley," I responded.

"We were both fucked up, Mel. Shit happens when you drink," he said.

At this point I started to grow hysterical. "Is that why something happened to Ashley, too?! She told me what you did to her!" I yelled.

He looked at me with his eyes wide open and threw his arms up and growled, "Fuck Ashley. She's a liar," he replied. "She opened a Human Resources case against me, and I got a write-up over that bitch! She texted me relentlessly and wanted me so bad. I showed Human Resources all of the messages, and they still gave me a write-up," he yelled.

I was grabbing my legs as the next question came out of my mouth. "What did Human Resources give you regarding the gala?" I asked, my voice sounding more calm.

Bradley made eye contact with me as he gritted his teeth. "They didn't give me shit. What I did to you at the gala was a hundred times worse than what that bitch claimed I did to her, and they didn't give me shit, Mel!"

I froze. *Is this really happening?* I thought. All of the feelings I'd tried to suppress started to come over me. I realized my hands were shaking. I wasn't sure if it was from anger or nervousness. "You didn't get a write-up or even a warning from the gala?" I asked.

"No I didn't, and another thing—"

Tears started to burn my eyes, but I continued to hold my composure. I was not going to give him any more power.

"Look at where you're at in life and look at where I'm at," he said.

I raised my eye brows as the tears started to flow down my cheek. "What do you mean by that?" I asked.

He moved two of his fingers up and down as shrugged his shoulders. "You're unemployed. 'Finding yourself.' Need I say another word?" he asked.

I started to feel sick. I wanted to throw up but it wasn't because of the alcohol that I had drunk this time. "Can I go upstairs?" I asked.

"Sure thing," he responded as he looked toward his dog. I walked up to his bathroom and forced myself to throw up. I heard Bradley knocking on the door.

"You okay in there?" he asked.

"Yes," I yelled back. I wiped the vomit from my mouth as I looked at myself in the mirror. My eyes looked empty, my face pale and my body felt frail. I managed to walk a few steps and unlock the door.

My hands were trembling as I moved the handlebar. Bradley was on the opposite side of the door looking at me with care in his eyes.

"Look, I'm sorry. I said some pretty fucked up things," he said.

"It's all good," I responded.

"Do you want to lie down?" he asked.

I decided to stay the night as I had been drinking and I couldn't drive home. There was something that was still inclining me to be around Bradley even after all the fucked up stuff that had just happened.

I lay down next to Bradley. Bradley turned his back and fell asleep. The conversation started circulating in my mind as I turned the opposite direction and tried to pass out.

A few hours later when I awoke, I was starving.

When I awoke, I was starving.

"I can make us breakfast," said Bradley.

"I would like that," I responded.

Bradley returned thirty minutes later with a bunch of food.

"Thank you for making me food," I said. I smiled but my eyes gave me away. Bradley looked at me and tried to manage a smile.

"I should be heading out. I have lunch plans with a few of my old clients from the bank. I'm sorry if I said anything that upset you last night," I said.

Bradley nodded his head and was looking toward the ground. "I'm sorry if I said anything too," he said.

I went to lunch and pretended like nothing was wrong. Once I got home my throat started to choke.

Mallory approached me. "What's wrong, Melissa?" she asked. I fell into her arms and broke out in a cry.

"Can I lie in your bed while you do schoolwork?" I asked.

I lay on Mallory's bed as she gently rubbed my back. I felt so comforted lying next to her. "Do you want food?" she asked.

"I don't have an appetite," I responded. After several hours I started to get a little bit of energy.

"I'm worried about you Mel," she said, I lifted my eyes up weakly.

"I don't know what's wrong with me? A part of me hates him and a part of me wants to be with him," I responded.

"Have you thought about seeing a therapist?" she asked.

"That's a good idea," I responded.

When I walked out of the room Skyler was sitting in the living room. He turned his head and his eyes looked full of concern. "Mel, can I speak to you?" he asked.

I nodded my head as my shoulders hung low and I sat on the couch. "I don't know why I allowed you to see Bradley on October second or why I allowed it last night. I couldn't stop thinking about you and felt sick to my stomach for not stopping you," he said.

I nodded my head as tears flowed from my eyes. "Thank you, Sky. I appreciate you caring about me," I said.

"I'm serious, Mel. I know I'm your tenant, but I'm also your friend. This is so wrong," he said.

I walked up to my room. I put the sheets over my head and felt empty. I slept until 10:30 am the next day. When I woke up I felt like I had been hit by a car. My body ached. I pulled out my phone and texted Bradley. As much as I hated the way he treated me I equally hated thinking about life without him. I felt trauma bonded. This individual had consumed me over the past three years and I didn't know how to let him go. I was a battered dog that continued to run back to her owner.

The last message I sent Bradley was on December 2, 2021. He never responded, and subconsciously I felt relieved. I wanted to believe so badly that Bradley was a good person. I wanted to pretend that I was never sexually assaulted by him. I thought that in order for me to have peace, I needed to get validation from the very person who had sexually assaulted me. *What would my father think?* continued to play in my mind as I looked at the ground and tears flowed to my eyes.

13

MEMORIES THAT LAST A LIFETIME

Everything seemed to be going wrong. In other words... I just had realized it was Valentine's Day. I booked an Airbnb, and they canceled on us, so we needed to find another spot. I dragged my feet to the car and looked at the droplets that were evolving into miniature basketballs falling outside. The last Valentine's Day that brought me happiness instead of dread was in 2015. Our clients would bring the cutest chocolates and make my employees feel special. On February 14, 2015, I was excited to work my typical day at the bank to see what surprises clients had for our team but I also felt sad. All of my friends had a partner and I was twenty-four years old and single. *When will I find my person? Is he out there?* I was sitting at my desk and saw someone bringing in the most beautiful flowers.

"I have a delivery for Melissa Work," said the flower man.

I looked down at the flowers and saw a card from my dad. I opened the card with my fingertips.

Will you be my Valentine?

Love,
Dad

My dad always knew how to make me feel special. All of my friends were posting sappy posts and I ended making a post of my own. I took a picture of the eccentric flowers my dad sent me and tagged my father on Facebook.

"This man never seizes to amaze me!"

#daddyslittlegirl #whyyouhavetomakethestandardasohigh #loveyoudad #youdabest#nomancompares #probwhyimstillsingle #luckiestgirlintheworld #valentinesday

I heard my phone ringing and saw that it was my dad. "How are you holding up honey?" asked my father. I paused for several seconds. "I'm fine," I responded. "Tell me the truth," said my father. My dad always knew when I was fibbing and I couldn't get one lie past him.

"I guess I'm a little upset," I said.

"What's wrong, honey?" asked my father.

"I feel like my dating life is the one thing I can't get right," I said.

"It is going to take an incredibly special man to date you. You my dear are the most special girl in this world. Sometimes I fear you don't see how amazing you are," said my father. "On an unrelated note, how are you enjoying the Lifetime movie?"

"How did you know I was watching Lifetime?!" I asked.

My father chuckled. "Sometimes I don't think you know how well I know you," said my father.

Now we were both laughing. "It's keeping me sane," I said.

"Try to get some rest after. I love you, honey," said my father.

I zoned out and came back to the present moment.

Lily moved her head toward the right to look in my direction. "We'll need to find another spot," said Lily. I started looking on booking.com and found a cute bed and breakfast that was 39 euros a night. When we arrived I saw a common area with couches, games, and lots of warm colorful paintings on the main wall. There was a covered outdoor area with a hammock and ping pong tables. There were dining room tables that filled the outside area and fake green grass on the ground. There were dogs and cats.

My favorite dogs name was Mr. Whiskey. Mr. Whiskey was a cream white color that was a mix between Labrador and a breed I couldn't identify. Mr. Whiskey could open the door to the living room that had a handle on it. Mr. Whiskey would jump up and move his paw in a hand like motion that made the door knob open. Lily took a video of this and I captured the moment on my social media. This dog was the most talented dog I have ever seen!

French people ate dinner every night at the bed and breakfast at 8 pm and would enjoy conversation until around 9:30 pm. I saw a French woman fixing a cabinet in the bed and breakfast. A man got up to help the woman. My father was always kind like this man. I always knew it, but the first time I realized that others knew it was when I went to Dominican Republic with two of my best friends Kingston and Chris during spring break. For my high school senior project my teacher approved me to provide assistance for a project that my father was funding to build small homes for people in need. It would be Kingston and Chris first time out of the country and we were all eager to embark on this journey together. In the morning we had to board my father's truck to get up the mountains. Juan introduced me as Mr. Work's daughter and the local Dominicans gave me a hug. An older lady named Nidia started to cry as she wrapped her arms around my shoulders. "You don't know how much your father has helped my family," said Nidia. I met a few other families who came up to me one by one. "Your father has changed our lives. For the first time in our life we have a home, a safe place that my children can feel secure," said Daniel.

I took a step forward and landed in mud. It was a hot Spring day and smelled like fertilizer. I wrapped my arms around Daniel's shoulders and in that moment no words needed to be said. Daniel held me in close for several seconds. He wiped his cheek with the palm of his hand. I felt so proud to call myself my father's daughter. Daniel wanted to give us a chicken as a form of gratitude. These families had so little—yet they wanted to offer anything they could.

Their children were playing without electronics but with each other. I learned what my dad had been trying to teach me in previous years. Happiness comes from within. "It's time to go," said Juan.

I looked out the window of the truck and in this moment I knew I wanted to make an impact in the world—I wanted to help others the way my father had. When I returned from this trip my eldest brother was deemed fully disabled. My mother, father, brother and I felt devastated over the news. My mother and father took care of my oldest brother full time and my mother did whatever she could to help my brother have as independent of a life as possible.

14

REFLECTION OVER THE
PAST FEW YEARS

November 15, 2021

It had been three years and seven months since my father had back surgery. Twelve months since Quincy and I broke up. Nine months since I left my corporate job. Six months since we concluded my father's lawsuit. Three months since I brought my father to the Mayo Clinic. Two months since I found out Harry was cheating on me, and nine days since I saw Bradley. Reflecting back on the last few years a whole hell of a lot had happened. I called my best friend Amy.

"Hello!" said Amy.

"Do you think it will ever end?" I asked.

"What?" asked Amy.

"The craziness that life continues to throw at me," I said.

"I think it has ended and life is starting to finally bless you," said Amy.

I got off the phone with Amy and started to think about this. I felt like maybe this was the ending of a beautiful beginning until November 22. I opened my Facebook account and saw that a few friends had written on my dear childhood friend's page and said, "Rest in Peace."

My brother had introduced me to Justin, who was quite the lady's man. Justin was four years older than me and two years older than my brother. We both looked up to Justin and admired him the same way. I remember the first time I laid eyes on Justin I was at the YMCA doing gymnastics. There was a small boy sitting on the side of the basketball court with his arms folded looking down. I saw Justin approach this boy and before you knew it the boy was smiling from ear to ear as Justin passed him the basketball. This is the type of man Justin was—he always wanted to include everyone, and had the ability to make each person feel special. Back then, I thought I'd met the love of my life. Ever since that day all of my closest childhood friends knew that I was forever in love with Justin Krafft.

This cannot be true. No this absolutely cannot be true. I continued to scroll through his Facebook and realized that it was in fact true. I was lying in bed at the time and I cried out what sounded like a yelping sound.

My friend looked mortified and asked, "What's happened, Melissa?!"

I couldn't come to terms with telling her that my dear Justin had passed away. The yelping sound turned into bawling. Courtney held me and didn't ask another question until I had calmed down. Justin passed away from a drug that was laced. I was angry. How could this happen to one of the best men I knew? I wrote to his mother and fell into depression the next week.

I was getting ready in the bathroom when *Who Am I?* By Bazzi started to play. When the chorus came on something took over my body. I had never heard this song before but yet the words related to me in so many ways. I looked in the mirror and I couldn't tell who the girl on the other side was. The words were ripping a Band-Aid off a large wound. A wound that no one else saw when they looked at me but was the only thing I could see when I looked at myself. My body ached and I fell to the ground. I covered my hands over my face and started to shake. I rested my face on the ground. *I just want this to end.*

I heard a knock on the bathroom door.

"Are you in there?" asked Skyler.

I heard a peep come out of my mouth. "Yes, I'll be out shortly," I responded.

"No worries. Take your time," said Skyler as his voice carried away.

I didn't want to move. I wanted to disappear. It had been a little over one year since I took Ativan, but all my mind could think about was numbing the pain. I grabbed the ground with my hands and forced myself up. My legs were trembling as I stood as straight as I could and walked to my gray cabinet in my room. As my hand shook I opened the drawer and grabbed the bottle of Ativan with my right hand. I started swirling the bottle and passed it over to my left hand. *You don't want to do this Melissa,* I thought. I opened the container with my right hand. I looked at the bottle with endless white pills. I held the bottle with my right hand and dumped two white pills into my left hand and swung it behind my mouth. Shortly after I felt all of the emotions released from my body. I took a deep breath in and out and went back to bed to rest my eyes.

I forced myself to leave my room and drive to my safe place: Multnomah Falls. While I was driving I saw a rainbow. It felt as if Justin was sending me a sign that I was going to be okay. I looked at the rainbow and felt comfort. For the first time in a week I felt a small piece of peace. I went back on Facebook and saw that there was a memorial organized by two of Justin's friends that was scheduled on December 11, 2021, at 2:00 pm. I dropped all of my plans for that weekend and let my parents know that I would be driving to my hometown of Medford to attend Justin's memorial. When Justin passed away, my mother and father were devastated. Justin had spent a lot of time at our home, and they adored him like a son.

My father said that he would like to write something on Justin's Facebook page. It took him seven hours to articulate what he would like to say. My mother and I helped my father and were patient with my father when he was getting his thoughts together. I watched my niece the weekend of Justin's memorial. My heart was heavy and my niece could tell.

"Tia, what's wrong?" asked my niece.

"One of my dear friends passed away. He was your Popa's best friend from childhood," I said.

"Is that why you are in town?" asked my niece.

"It's one of the main reasons. The other reason is to see my beautiful girl," I said. I touched her nose gently and kissed her cheek.

She started to giggle.

"I'm sorry you lost a friend."

My niece reached out for my hand.

Justin had so many people who loved him. His biggest desire in life was to meet a nice woman and have a family. He would have been so happy with the basic things in life. I remember one day I was crying over a boy. Justin put his arm around my shoulders. "Are you ready to shoot some shots?" asked Justin.

I felt the pavement below my feet, and as I threw the ball I heard Justin's voice echoing, "Mayla Work, WNBA star!"

The basketball swooshed as I turned my head to see a smile ear to ear. Justin never wanted anyone to feel sad and put others' needs ahead of himself. A few hours later my brother told me that Justin's girlfriend broke up with him. I hadn't realized that Justin had gone through a breakup recently himself.

When I arrived at Justin's memorial, I felt heavy. I looked like I hadn't slept in weeks. I walked through the front door and saw Justin's twin sister and mother. I introduced myself to Justin's mother and right when she saw me she gave me a big hug.

"I don't know if you remember who I am," I said.

"Of course I remember who you are, Melissa. Come here, dear," said Kaisa.

I wrapped my arms around her neck and rested my face in her shoulder. I couldn't imagine the pain she was going through and here she was providing me comfort.

The memorial was beautiful. I could hear Justin's favorite tunes—which were my favorite songs also. Changes by Tupac played and I remember the countless nights Justin, my brother and I would shoot hoops and talk about life. Justin would dribble the ball back in a quick V like motion and shoot from the three-point line. Like clockwork the ball would swoosh and I would stand with my mouth wide open.

A small piece of me kept thinking Justin would come around the corner and start doing his capacious dance moves that everyone knew and loved. There were several people that spoke at Justin's memorial. One of them was Justin's best friend Travis. Travis loved Justin as a brother. When he spoke to the audience you could hear the pain in his voice. I looked to the right and saw Travis's beautiful girlfriend crying. The pain in her eyes made me cry more. How could Justin be gone? I still didn't want to believe that my sweet J had left this earth. Justin's mother grabbed the microphone. "Would anyone else like to speak?" asked Kaisa.

 I stood up and walked to the front as my hands shook.

"Justin was more than a friend to me. He was like my big brother. I remember one day when I was crying over a boy that didn't like me. Justin looked down into my eyes and said, 'You are going to meet the most special man in this world that deserves you. You are one of a kind.' He provided me comfort when I needed it most." I walked back to my seat and wiped the tears from my eyes.

Justin had an addiction. An addiction that he ran to because he was hurt where he was at in life. A pain that so many of us experience but his Band-Aid of choice was drugs. Justin got clean and relapsed. If life gave him more time—I'm confident he would have beat his addiction.

I reached out to Justin's mom shortly after. The bond that Justin shared with his mom was similar to the bond my father and I shared. It brought me comfort knowing that I could communicate with Justin's mom and build on our relationship. I reached out to Kaisa to get her blessing to write some of my favorite memories of Justin in my book. I shared with Kaisa my desire to forgive my father's surgeon so that I could finally be at peace.

Kaisa shared with me a few of Justin's dreams and that Justin had lived with her the last year and a half of his life. "Justin lived with me for a year and a half before he died. He and I became closer than ever. We would stay up all night and talk about anything and everything. Our bond was very strong. He shared so much with me during that time. I feel very blessed to have had this experience with him. The thing that confuses me so much is that Justin struggled with loneliness, pretty intensely at times, and yet so many people loved him. He also wanted a girlfriend and partner so badly. He ached for a relationship.

"He always said he had to straighten out his life first. I would hear him talk for hours about his dream for a mate, and to have kids. He truly wanted the simple basic things. I have no doubt he would have made the greatest dad. He was always incredible with little kids. Forgiveness can be tough. Well actually it can be painfully difficult, but I have learned it is the only way to be truly free. Also forgiving ourselves," said Kaisa.

After Justin's memorial I knew I wanted to make a change in my life and begin my healing.

15

CLAIRA, FRANCE

February 15, 2022

Lily and I arrived to La Petit Moka at the local mall for breakfast. The food was very affordable. I stopped the first waitress I could find. "Do you speak English?" I asked.

The waitress rolled her eyes and spoke to us in French. *I'm going to take that as a no and need to learn basic French ASAP!* I thought to myself.

I saw that the breakfast place had crepes and knew that to be a French thing. What do I want to order? Crepes! My pronunciation was "crapes" because that's how I always pronounced it in the USA.

"If you call crepes 'crapes,' they will be very offended. How you are saying it sounds like a mix between crap and crepe," said Lily.

"I had no idea," I said.

Lily put up her hands to emphasize the next point she was about to make. "The French are very proud people, so you do not want to piss them off," said Lily.

When the waitress delivered our crepes, she had eased up and was smiling. She asked me a question, and for whatever reason I said, "Oui."

 "You are saying yes to everything," said Lily.

"I don't know any other words," I said.

Lily broke out in laughter.

I had an inner thought about how this is real growth for me, not being afraid, saying yes to everything! When I tried my first bite of the crepe my lips started watering and I felt a sensation coming from inside me. When Lily and I got back to the bed and break-fast I saw an older woman with white hair, a cane and small dog next to her side. "Do you speak English?" asked the old woman. I nodded. Evelyn looked into the distance as her voice started to wonder off.

"I love that you are traveling with your friend. When I was younger I remember doing a similar trip as you two and meeting a nice young lady that became one of my best friends. We lost contact through the years because I moved and she moved but I will forever be grateful for crossing paths with her," said Evelyn.

I looked at Evelyn intently. She was still looking off into the dis-tance. "Where did you travel to?" I asked.

Evelyn met my eyes and smiled from ear to ear. "We met in Santiago, Chile. I took a three-month trip and originally traveled to the South of Chile by myself. I made a map of where I wanted to go. This was before smartphones and Google Maps, you had to do things the old school way, which I loved. I would decorate my map and make it exciting! I marked all of the places I wanted to go," said Evelyn.

"How did you meet your friend?" I asked.

"I met my friend on a bus when I was traveling in Chile. We both decided we wanted to see Bolivia and Argentina. We ended our travels in Argentina and she went off to Peru and I went back to Barcelona, where I lived for many years," said Evelyn.

"That's incredible! How long ago was this?" I asked.

"It feels like a lifetime ago, but it was twenty years ago, when I was sixty. My friend was forty years old," said Evelyn.

"I hope that when I'm sixty years old I can still travel the world like you," I said.

Evelyn chuckled. "I'm sure you will. Once you have the travel bug you never really lose it. What I love about you girls is that you are seeing the world and learning new cultures. Many people get stuck in their ways and never learn new things. The world is so big, so beautiful and there is so much to see." Evelyn moved her finger up and down. "Please do not ever lose your desire to learn new things. The best experiences I have had in my life have been from traveling, and some of the people I met along the way have become like family. You will find that it will happen for you to."

Evelyn's dog jumped up in Lily's lap. Evelyn's dog was named Nana. Nana had beautiful big brown eyes, white and light brown hair and whiskers that dangled from her chin.

"Would it be all right if I shared a little piece of your story in my book?" I said.

"I would love that," said Evelyn.

When we left, I wrapped my arms around Evelyn's neck. She welcomed my gesture and gave me a tight squeeze. Lily and I went to the crepes spot and saw the same waitress that served us. This time she was smiling from ear to ear. We ordered our favorite sugar crepes and it was just as good as the first time. We went to the grocery store to grab lunch. I needed to buy a needle and thread as my only warm jacket was starting to fall apart. My jacket had traveled through many adventures with me. Starting with when my father bought it for me from JC Penney, to winter storms in Portland, to date nights, and now to Europe. Wearing it reminded me of my dad, and I felt safe.

My jacket needed to serve me on a spontaneous trip Lily and I were about to take in four days.

16

ALMALFI COAST

February 24, 2022

I had seen the day earlier that conflict was escalating in Ukraine and Russia. As I opened the news I saw that Russia had officially invaded Ukraine. *What?* I felt sick to my stomach. I cannot believe that there is a new war that is beginning in 2022. *Haven't we learned anything from our past?!* I thought. I felt as if I might throw up and needed to wake Lily up even though it was the crack of dawn.

"Lily! Wake up!" I said.

Lily turned her back around, still half asleep. "What is it?!" asked Lily.

"Russia has officially gone into Ukraine and launched missiles. I cannot believe that is happening," I said.

 I continued to check my phone every ten minutes and couldn't think of anything else. The world was watching Ukraine being attacked and the president of Ukraine pleaded with the world leaders to help him. I received several calls from family and friends.

"Are you coming back to the states with everything that is going on?" Ann asked. It was devastating what was happening before my eyes. I felt so sorry for the people of Ukraine. I continued to watch the news diligently. The news would predict whether I had to cut my travels short or continue on my journey.

I took a walk to try to figure out what to do. I decided to take a bus to explore Villa Rufolo. I spent 2 euros to get there by bus, and when I arrived I could see the whole Almalfi Coast. I was on top of the world. The water was glistening and was the deepest blue I had ever seen. I got off the bus and looked toward my left to see a little girl on her father's shoulders.

When I was six, I would go to the grocery store with my father and I would sit on my father's shoulders and use his ears to steer. I would turn one ear and he would walk in that direction.

Sometimes I would navigate him to walk into an aisle and start laughing if he did. I would navigate him to go take a hard left to run into a food piece in the aisle then shift his ear toward the right to walk down the middle the aisle. This game made me love going to the grocery store with my dad. Anytime my dad would say "I'm going to the grocery store!" I would yell, "I'm coming, Popa!"

Seeing the little girl laugh with her father brought me happiness—it also made me sad. I miss my father so much. I would do anything to have his health back and get one more chance to speak to him about life, hear his advice on business and or play a card game. Tears started rolling down my cheek. As sad as I felt in this moment I equally felt blessed to remember the feeling of how happy this memory made me. I wanted to take this journey to forget the sorrows of my life, and here I am changed—because through remembering the pain, I also felt blessed for the first time.

I met a guy named Sheek from Israel. I couldn't take my eyes away from his. When he asked me to go on a hike the next day, I said yes. I hadn't had a date in so long, my romantic life had been such a mess, but I could I do this! I woke up at 7:00 am and started getting ready. I wore my lululemon hiking pants and a new black sweater that I had purchased. I started walking down to the bus stop and when I got to the ticket booth I asked the employee what bus stop I would need to get off at to prepare for our hike. "I'm sorry but there was a landslide on the trail so we closed the path," said the employee.

Sheek would be here any minute. I texted Sheek. "We'll find something else to do!" responded Sheek. I saw Sheek walking down the road he was wearing black pants, White Nikes and a white sweatshirt that made him look tan. He looked even more handsome than what I remembered.

"You haven't been to Positano right?" asked Sheek.

I heard a voice come out my mouth that sounded unfamiliar to me. "I have not," I responded as my lip trembled. *Why am I so nervous?!* I thought.

"It looks like the next bus takes off at 10:45 am. Want to get a coffee and get to know each other better?" asked Sheek. Positano was one hour away from Almalfi, and I was nervous that I might get motion sick on the bus. I told Sheek.

"I'll help you however I can," said Sheek.

I felt safe around him and that felt refreshing. We started talking about life and what brought us to Almalfi. I shared my condensed story about my father, breaking up with my ex-boyfriend and how I wanted to get out of my comfort zone to heal my soul.

Writing while traveling provided me comfort. Each stroke of the pen felt freeing as I unraveled a new page that has made me into the woman I am today. I was determined to finish my story from start to finish and realized my favorite time of day was when I had a pen in my hand or heard the endless clicks on my laptop. Writing about something so tragic actually made me feel stronger, better, and more in tune with the world.

We went to a restaurant on the beach in Positano. The sun was beaming on the water and my skin felt warm. Sheek and I ordered wine and a salad to split. We walked around the town until we decided to try a new restaurant and enjoy the views. Sheek grabbed my hand and we ran to a beautiful viewpoint to catch the sunset. We sat down hand in hand and watched in silence. Sheek pulled out his phone and started to play Cold Play. We both started to sing along holding hands until the night got dark.

I hadn't realized how much time had pass. "What time is the last bus to Almalfi?" I asked. Sheek looked down at his watch as he grabbed my hand and we started to run toward the bus stop. We made the last bus with three minutes to spare. I rested my head on Sheek's shoulder and felt safe. I realized my view on men was changing and that I started to feel like the old me that trusted more easily. I looked out the window as a smile approached my lips.

17

OHRID, MACEDONIA

March 25, 2021

L ily and I arrived in Ohrid, Macedonia. We sat down at a restaurant that overlooked the Macedonia flag. A small orange kitten jumped on my lap. I'm allergic to cats but this one was particularly special. I couldn't resist petting her. She purred gently and snuggled up in my lap. The cat got up and jumped into Lily's lap. She started snuggling with Lily. We ordered another round of wine. Red for me and white for Lily.

As the night progressed I started to get attached to this cat. "How hard do you think it would be to bring a cat to the United States?" I asked.

We started looking at the embassy guidelines and saw that it wasn't too difficult. "If we bring the cat home, then you have to bring her to the United States," said Lily.

I looked at her eyes and saw the seriousness she held. I nodded my head. Lily and I asked the staff at the restaurant if she was a stray.

"She would love a home," said the waitress.

Lily held the kitten tightly in her arms as we got home. The kitten got comfortable and roamed around the apartment. She snuggled close to Lily and fell asleep on Lily's stomach. I started sneezing throughout the night and realized that sure enough I still have horrible allergies to cats. The next morning my face was puffy and my sinuses were congested. Lily and I looked up the veterinarian office to see where we could get our kitten vaccinated and the documents needed to show she's had her shots. We found a nice vet named Tony.

"I can't believe I'm doing this," I said as I looked toward Lily. The vet finished up with our kitten and I purchased a kennel, food, and a leash.

As we walked outside Lily was holding our kitten. On our way to the car the kitten jumped out of Lily's arms and out of her leash. She started to run.

"Oh no!" screamed Lily. "Melissa, try to grab her!"

I ran toward the kitten, but she was too fast.

She ran underneath one of the cars behind the fire department. Lily and I started looking under the cars to locate her.

"Score! I found her!" I said.

Lily looked relieved for one moment and could see her tail hanging. Lily tried to grab her without any luck. After an hour of doing this we sat by the car. I saw something run. "Oh shit. She just got out," I yelled.

Lily jumped up and we both looked but couldn't find the kitten.

"How can I help you ladies?" asked one of the firemen. We told him the story and he looked at us with concern in his eyes.

"If you hear anything, can you call me on WhatsApp?" I asked.

"Of course. I will let my coworkers know as well," he said kindly.

Lily and I stayed there for a few hours looking diligently, with no luck. "I'm sure they'll call us if they find her," I said to try to make Lily feel better. "She may even go back to the restaurant since she goes there every day," I said. I didn't feel as confident as the words were flowing out of my mouth because the vet office was a ten-minute drive from the restaurant, and we had to pass a busy intersection to get there. I squeezed Lily's shoulder.

Lily looked toward the ground and started to cry. I rubbed her back. "The last time I felt this sad was when my brother passed away," she said. My eyes got big as I looked at her. "Here's our kitten all alone in this world and it's because I didn't hold onto her tight enough. I had no idea she would run," said Lily.

I continued to rub her back. "It could have happened to anyone," I said.

Lily's shoulders started to shake as she put her hands over her eyes. "I failed her and I failed you. You just paid for all of her shots," Lily said.

I started to shake my head. "You did not fail me, and you could have never known. She was so calm at the vet's," I said as I continued to rub Lily's back.

"We'll find her," I said confidently.

"She's gone, Melissa. Just like my brother. She's gone," said Lily.

We drove back home and didn't say another word. I felt heavy from seeing Lily so upset. Lily and I decided to extend our stay in Ohrid, Macedonia, for an extra week to look for our kitten. We went to the same restaurant each evening in hopes that the kitten would come back. We walked through dark alleys and looked underneath every trash can. We saw many cats but unfortunately none was our cat.

Lily grabbed my shoulder and looked into my eyes. "If we find her, can I take her back to the Netherlands with me?" asked Lily.

I was relieved to hear this, as I hadn't realized how bad my allergies would act up. "Of course," I responded as I held Lily's shoulder tightly. After six days we had no luck and had to continue on our journey to Theft, Albania.

18
____

ALBANIA

April 1, 2022

"Melissa! You would never believe!" said Lily.

I turned my shoulder to face Lily with my eyes attempting to open.

"The waitress texted me back from the restaurant and said the kitten is back!" said Lily.

"Does she know it's our cat for sure?" I asked.

"She's a hundred percent confident!" said Lily.

I felt like five pounds had been lifted from my shoulders and a tingle ran through my body. "What are you going to do?!" I asked.

"I will drive to Ohrid in two days when we depart Albania! If the cat is still there, then it was meant to be!" said Lily.

I saw a tear appear in Lily's eyes. "I am so happy for you," I said.

"This is the best birthday present I could have ever asked for!" responded Lily.

"Happy birthday!" I smiled as I saw Lily opening her eyes slowly. "I cannot wait to celebrate tonight!" I said.

Lily and I started packing our things and thanked the host. I gave her a hug and held her tight. She couldn't speak one word of English and I could only say "Thank you" in Albanian. Yet I felt so close to her after spending four days at Bujtina Polia in Theft, Albania. There was a tremendous amount of snow that had fallen the evening before. Lily didn't have snow tires and on top of that her car was all wheel drive.

"Do you think we're making it out of here?" I asked.

"We have no other option but to try," said Lily.

We approached behind a snow plow and I felt relieved. There were three men sitting in the snow plow. "Oh no," said Lily. I heard the car's engine revving, trying to push as hard as it could, but we came to a complete stop.

"Try to back up," I said. I saw the snow plow backing up. *Thank goodness for our guardian angels*, I thought.

A worker strapped a big cable to the front of Lily's car and behind the snow plow. "We are going to pull you. There is no other way you're making it up to the top of this hill," he yelled.

They started to drive and I felt my body lurch with each yank on the cable. I turned to look at Lily and saw that she was trembling. I grabbed her hand. "We are getting out of here," I said.

Shortly after I saw that there was snow blocking the road. Lily put the car in park and we got out of the car. I turned around and saw there were five cars behind us. "We have another snow plow that will help get us out of here!" he yelled to the bystanders. We all stood together watching our heroes in awe, knowing that we would be leaving by the good grace of these men.

We waited patiently as Lily passed out a few snacks to the men helping us. I took a video of the snow plow working diligently. They were able to move the snow to open up the road. Lily and I got back into the car and the guys continued to pull us up the road with the cable. Lily had told one of the bystanders where we were staying in Shkodër, Albania. He was handsome and looked at Lily with lust. We arrived in Shkodër four hours after starting our journey, which should have lasted one hour under normal weather conditions. I took Lily out for a nice dinner. The waiter sang "Happy Birthday" and brought Lily a cake. The waiter handed a sheet of paper that had a phone number on it. "Someone wanted you to have this," the waiter said.

"I'm going to text him!" said Lily.

Thirty minutes later we were on our way to meet the man who fancied Lily. He picked us up in a Land Rover. "I own a few rentals at the hotel you are staying at. I hope you enjoy your stay there!" he said.

"Do you have any single cute friends?" I asked.

"Why?" he responded as he smiled.

"I'm trying not to be a third wheel," I responded as I shrugged my shoulders.

Lily looked embarrassed. "You're not!" she said.

"Let me text a few of my friends," he said.

Fifteen minutes later his friend was walking through the door. He couldn't speak a word of English, but we were gesturing to one another with our arms, and I laughed to myself thinking how silly we looked.

"You guys want to go to a dance club?" asked Adam.

"I'm down!" I responded.

All four of us were off and went to the club. "Let's take some shots!" said the guy.

Lily and I started to dance the night away. We had four shots at this point and I started to feel dizzy but was having too much fun to notice.

I went outside to call my best girlfriend. "Just in case something happens to me, here's a screen shot of this guy's Instagram," I said.

"Melissa, get home. You're drunk," she responded.

"Melissa!" I heard Lily yelling my name and turned around. "Where did you go?!" she asked.

"Sorry, I was talking to Amy," I responded.

"You ready to go home?" she asked. We started to walk.

"I'll give you girls a ride," said Adam.

"Oh no, I'm not getting into your car when you've been drinking!" said Lily sternly.

"I agree with Lily. We'll walk," I said.

We started to walk, and Adam yelled back: "Are you worried about the police?!"

Lily turned around.

"The police don't care here! You want to see?!" he said.

Lily and I watched him walk across the street, and to our surprise we saw two armed officers. He started waving his arms and motioned for us to come over. We casually walked over.

"I just asked them if I could drive and they don't care! See," said Adam.

"I don't care if they don't care. I do!" said Lily.

I felt dizzy but was watching the body language that Lily, Adam, the officers and Adam's friend Paul were giving.

The officer looked at Lily. "Would it help if we gave you a ride, ma'am?" asked the officer.

Lily nodded her head and grabbed my hand. "We'll follow behind you!" said Adam. I got into the police van behind one of the officers, and Lily followed me.

I was sitting in the middle between Lily and the officer. The other officer was driving the vehicle. I turned to Lily and made a facial expression. I was curious why one of the officers sat next to me and not in front with his coworker. The hotel was only a six-minute drive away, and as the officer started driving I felt a hand rubbing against my leg gently. I looked down and turned my head to face Lily. I motioned with my fingers to my leg so she could see what was happening.

"Do not touch her there!" said Lily.

The officer looked at her with surprise and placed his right hand in front of him. I froze. "She may be drunk, but I am very sober!" said Lily.

The other officer proceeded to drive down the road and the officer started to rub my leg again and started to make his way down.

I looked at Lily with despair.

"Don't touch her there!" Lily growled.

I wanted to say something—to get anything out of my mouth, but I was frozen. This feeling felt too familiar.

The other officer looked in his rearview mirror and didn't say a word. "Sorry," the officer sitting next to me said casually. The officer pulled the van over.

Thank goodness, I see our hotel, I thought.

As Lily tugged my arm to get out of the van, the officer grabbed my face with both of his hands. I moved my head quickly and missed his tongue within a matter of inches as Lily tugged my arm.

"What the fuck is wrong with you?!" she growled at the officer. We rushed inside the hotel, where we looked at one another.

"What just happened?" I asked Lily.

"The officer was all over you!" she responded.

"Thank you for standing up for me. I have no idea why I froze," I said.

"You did nothing wrong. I can't believe that just happened."

I looked down and hadn't realized my hands were trembling. "I should have said something," I responded.

"What an animal," said Lily.

What is the common denominator between two of the most violating experiences of my life? Alcohol. *Thank goodness for Lily*, I thought.

Lily and I woke up early and gave each other a hug goodbye. Lily was off to Ohrid, Macedonia, to find the kitten, and I was headed to Kotor, Montenegro, to start the rest of my journey alone.

"It's not goodbye, but I'll see you soon," said Lily.

I looked into Lily's eyes and smiled. "Thank you," I said.

"For what?" asked Lily.

"For the last two and a half months. I needed you," I said.

Lily and I held each other tightly for the next few minutes. The rain was coming down hard. My hair was drenched and water was dripping onto my jacket. I wrapped my hand around my handle and readjusted my backpack and started to run to the bus stop.

19

TIME TO TRAVEL ALONE

I got off the bus with my luggage, backpack, and a plastic bag to hold the rest of my things I had accumulated over the trip. My feet were soaked. My hair hung damply over my face and I stared at my phone diligently to find the studio. Thirty-nine steps up the cobblestone road until I arrived at the teal bedroom door that would be my home for the next week. There were shutters that blocked the sun from entering the room. I walked over to the shutters and opened the left one first, then used my fingertips to open the right one. The sun entered the room and I relaxed on the bed. I had met a friend on the bus named David who invited me to go on a scooter with him in two days. I've always wanted to ride a scooter and David was nice.

When we arrived one of the owners was using a screwdriver to screw something into the scooter. My stomach started to turn. The man looked me up and down twice and asked, "Have you ever rode a scooter?" he asked. "Once when I was a girl," I said. He moved his hand over his hair and started to scratch his head. "That's a problem. The last few tourist wrecked two scooters and you have to have experience to ride," he said. "Can I try?" asked

David. David attempted to ride the scooter and couldn't stop it fast enough. "That's it," said the man. I can rent you a car but not a scooter for liability purposes.

David and I drove back to the old town and parked the car. "I heard Ladder of Kotor has a beautiful view from the top," he said. "How far is the hike?" I asked. "It shouldn't be too hard," he said. We made our way up the trail and I started to feel tired. "I'm going to meet up with you once you're done. I have never been a good hiker and I hate slowing people down," I said. I walked back to my room with my shoulders hung over my feet.

When I awoke the next morning I took a hot shower. I rubbed the cheap soap on my legs. I watched the bubbles go into the drain and sat still for several minutes. I knew it was time to push myself and accomplish this hike. I put on my hiking shoes, workout pants and a plain white sweater. I arrived to the beginning of Ladder of Kotor and start walking up the steep stairs. My heart started to beat faster and sweat dropped down my face. Step by Step I told myself. I looked up at the top. I could turn around now. No one would know but I realized in this moment I would know. For the first time in my life I didn't want to do this for anyone but me. My nose was running, and the rocks were shuffling with each footstep I took. It sounded like someone rustling a Doritos bag. Step by step is the only thing I continued to tell myself as I moved forward. I started panting. *Step by step*, I thought. I made it to the top of the mountain and took a seat to enjoy the view. I smiled from ear to ear. "You made it!" I looked at the sunset and took a deep breath out and lay on the ground as I lay down to look at the sky.

I know I said I would wait to write Sam, but I couldn't resist. I mustered the courage on March 24—and we started texting every day. "Can I call you this weekend?" asked Sam. *Why am I so nervous?* I thought. The gentle expression of his voice made me feel calm. I poured myself some wine to calm my nerves as we started to talk. "Are you going to the bathroom?" asked Sam.

I started to chuckle. "Well, now I'm embarrassed," I responded.

We ended up talking on the phone for three hours. *I can't remember the last time I did that with someone!* I thought. I realized that I was starting to relate to a better kind of man than before I started this trip. Sam and I made plans to meet up for a date when I returned to the United States, and I was dying with anticipation!

I was walking to my Airbnb after eating at a restaurant listening to "Fantasy" by Mariah Carey. I felt happiness erupt through my body as I skipped down the cobblestone road and swirled. I started to sing "Fantasy" out loud as I moved my hands down my hips. *I must look so ridiculous right now*, I thought. A couple pointed at me and smiled. The girl started dancing to the song I was singing, and I heard a laugh come out of my mouth. I continued to dance to the beat, and it felt so good. I felt sexy. I felt powerful. I felt free. I started to move my arms in a wave like motion as Mariah Carey sang in the background. I moved my hands up and down next to my heart as Mariah sang "My heart beats faster." I skipped and did another twirl.

⸻⬦⸻

The day after, I was off to Dubrovnik, Croatia, on a bus. I watched the waves tumble over the rocks as they moved left, right, up and down. I noticed some of the water sparkled and seemed calm while other parts of the water were rough and turbulent. It was in this moment I understood what caused me to pursue Bradley. The feeling I tried so hard to understand over the last few years. The feeling that I hated more than anything within my bones but it kept smacking me in the face like waves in the ocean. I was trying to fight for Bradley so that I could "pretend" like I wasn't the girl who was sexually assaulted. If we were together it would make this situation worth it. I realized the day I got on an airplane to take this trip was the day I decided to fight for myself. My nails were bare, my face had no concealer, my mind felt clear, and I felt beautiful.

I saw a bird on the rock. The bird was by itself. The bird flew upwards then flew downwards toward the water—my heart stopped for a split second. I saw the bird glaze the water and fly directly up in a straight line as if nothing could faze it. The bird looked beautiful. It looked free. It had power and elegance to it. I turned my head around and smiled as I walked back to my Airbnb. I looked in my backpack and saw a bottle of Ativan with over ten white pills and another bottle labeled Adderall, with roughly twenty pills. I carried it around as a safety net in case I needed it. *I am not going to take it. I've come too far*, I thought.

I ordered a nice steak fillet and some red wine to treat myself for how far I'd come.

"Here you go, madam," said the waiter as he smiled. "You are beautiful."

I started to blush as I look down at my plate. "Thank you," I responded.

"Would you like to go on my scooter to see the most beautiful view over Dubrovnik tomorrow?" he asked.

I was skeptical at first, but then I thought: *It's time to start trusting men again.*

"When?" I asked. I looked into his eyes and he seemed genuine and kind.

The next day I was on his scooter, resting my hand on the handlebars. I felt the air hit my face as my hair flew behind me. It felt freeing. The waiter drove me back home and gave me a hug.

"Thank you," I said.

———◆———

I gathered my things to walk twenty-three minutes to start my ten-hour journey to Bled, Slovenia. I looked in the mirror and smiled. Here I was no make-up and I felt the most beautiful that I have in years. I heard "No Regrets" by Dappy on Spotify this reminded me of December 15 when I heard "Who am I" by Bazzi. The woman I was on December 15, 2021, to the woman I was right now felt like a lifetime ago. The growth I experienced as I grinned ear to ear is a feeling I will never forget.

"We're taking off to Zahreb," yelled the bus driver.

I stood up, swung my back pack over my shoulder and grabbed my overpacked blue bag to wheel behind me. My shoulders hung high as I managed to lift my blue bag over the stairs.

We arrived to Zagreb, Croatia, at 4:30 pm. *Shit*, I thought. The ticket I'd purchased to Ljubljana left at 4:15 pm. I ran to FlixBus. I saw on the side it said "Ljubljana."

"Excuse me. Do you speak English?" I asked the bus driver.

"Ticket," he responded. He looked unengaged as I scurried to find the ticket on my phone. "You're late. You need to buy a new ticket," he responded.

I walked to the ticket stadium and filled it out automatically. I bought a new ticket. I had twenty minutes!

I'm going to get some food at the shop! I thought. I ordered a pizza and a drink and scurried to find my money. I was holding my bus ticket in my left hand, cell phone in my right hand and attempting to use two of my fingers to grab some extra cash out of my backpack. *I look like a shit show*, I thought. A lady held the door open for me as I dragged my two bags and held my pizza. My pizza fell on the ground and my backpack hung over my shoulders as I attempted to grab it. She looked at me in disgust. *Three second rule*, I thought. I rushed over to my bus exit.

The same driver was grinning from ear to ear. "You made it." He chuckled.

No thanks to you, I thought. I attempted to smile as I threw my luggage underneath the bus. *I'm starting to get the hang of this!* I thought.

"Passport control," announced the bus driver. He pointed to me. "You first," he said.

"You want my passport?" I asked.

"No funny one, go down to the police officer," he said.

I had already been through quite a few borders but this never got old. "Stamp please?!" I asked the officer with a smile.

"No stamp for you," he replied. He then started chuckling. "Of course you get a stamp!" he said. I was excited to secure my first Slovenia stamp. I had three more buses to take before I made it to Bled, and I was adamant about not turning on my Wi-Fi. I had downloaded the offline maps and felt confident I could get to my hostel.

I grabbed the handlebar as I got off my last bus and landed in Bled. *Where next?* I thought. I walked to a bar next door so I could secure Wi-Fi and make sure I was going to the right place. *A twenty-eight-minute walk. Not bad*, I thought.

I started to walk and a rough-looking man pulled up his SUV next to me. He started motioning his arms to get in and moved his hand forward as if to tell me he would give me a ride.

"I speak English," I said. I shook my finger no and continued to move forward.

"I'll take you," he yelled.

"No thank you." I waved my hand, motioning for him to leave. I continued to walk and noticed that his car was sitting in the same spot. I pretended to call my friend and looked at his license plate. I saw his lights turn on as he drove past me. *Phew*, I thought as I continued on my way.

Shortly after, I saw a man I'd noticed earlier on the bus. It was dark and I was using my phone's flashlight on my path. "Hello! Where are you headed?" he asked.

"I am heading to a hostel twenty minutes away," I responded.

"Me too!" he said. He had a good demeanor about him, and that made me trust him instantly. After several minutes we realized that we were going to the same hostel. My legs started to get tired.

"What's your name?" he asked.

"Melissa," I responded. "What about yours?"

"Rico," he said. He gave me a warm smile. "Let me help you with that," said Rico.

We arrived to our hostel shortly after. As I was resting my eyes, the door creaked.

"It's been a long journey!" said a man.

"You'll be in bed two below this young lady," said the employee.

The man moved his shoulders up and down as his large backpack fell to the ground. "What a journey it's been," said the man.

"What brought you to Slovenia?" I asked with curiosity.

"I am traveling the world for the next two years. I figured it was now or never as I'm seventy years old," responded the man.

"What's your name?" I asked.

"You can call me Bonkers."

My eyes rose with even more curiosity. I felt safe with Bonkers and Rico, and it was lights out.

20

BLED, SLOVENIA

April 16, 2022

The wind was pushing the canoe backward. "One-two-three paddle," said Rico. My arms were exhausted and I was panting. "Keep pushing, Melissa. You can do this."

I continued to look forward and paddle with all my strength. I had a flashback to September 5, 2019, when I used all of my force to push Bradley off me and he pulled into me deeper.

"One-two-three paddle!" said Rico.

I started to count out loud with him.

"We are going faster! Keep up the momentum!" said Rico.

As I paddled forward I felt stronger. I started to get more energy and looked toward the beginning of where we rented our canoe. "One-two-three," I yelled, moving my body forward and backward to give me more strength.

Riko and I got the swing of it, and in no time we made it back.

"How was it?! The water looked rough out there!" said the employee.

"It was freeing," I responded. I looked into the lake and a smile approached my lips. *I am strong*, I thought.

Rico and I started walking down the road to go to the main town center of Lake Bohinj. I smelled gardenias as the mountains surrounded the ground we walked. The next day I hadn't noticed that I didn't need to use my phone's GPS to walk the twenty-seven minutes to the town center. I started to get familiar with where things were and only had Wi-Fi when I was in my hostel. Wi-Fi is a luxury that I didn't need 24/7. In fact, it felt freeing to not have connection with the outside world throughout the day.

"What brought you across the world?" asked Bonkers.

I started to talk about my story with Bonkers and Rico. I was surprised how comfortable I felt telling them about some of the most intimate details in my life.

"I would knock him out!" growled Bonkers.

Rico looked intently at the ground. "I am so sorry that happened to you Melissa," said Rico.

I could tell there was something that happened to bring Rico on this trip but wanted to wait until he was comfortable sharing it with me.

"Do you want a shot of whiskey?" asked Bonkers.

I shook my head no. "I'm sticking to red wine and nothing else!" I responded.

I got my things ready to leave for Munich, Germany. Bonkers grabbed my shoulders lightly. "Can I give you one piece of advice?" he asked as he looked intently into my eyes.

"Yes," I responded. He rubbed my shoulder gently. "We all came into this world equal and we are all leaving this world equal. Never think for one moment that someone is above you," he said.

These words struck a chord as I realized I had looked at Bradley above me over the last few years. I grabbed Bonkers for a hug. "Thank you for everything," I responded.

I walked 30 minutes to the bus station in Bled, Slovenia. The bus was leaving at 10:50 am to go to Munich.

"Can I buy a bus ticket here?" I asked.

"You have to do it on the Flix Bus app," said the employee.

"Can I sign onto the Wi-Fi?" I asked. She put the Wi-Fi password in my phone and I downloaded the application.

"It says it's sold out. Do you think I can pay for a ticket when I get on the bus?"

She started to chuckle. "Absolutely not," she responded.

I booked a ticket to Ljubljana, Slovenia. I had no idea where I would be going but thought I'd have better chances to get out of a central location.

Once I arrived, I found Wi-Fi and started searching for tickets. *Damn, there are no more tickets to Munich tonight*, I thought. I saw that there was a bus ticket available to Salzburg, Austria, and it would arrive at midnight. *Score! I just need to cancel the hotel I booked at Munich*, I thought. There was only one problem: I couldn't make international calls from my phone.

"Can I use your phone to call a hotel in Germany by chance?"

The waiter looked at me kindly. "Absolutely!" he responded.

"No refunds, madam," said the employee.

Well, there goes forty euros, I thought. I made my way back to the bus to wait the next six hours.

I took a bite of my burger and heard a ding. I saw that Rico had messaged me. "I'm so thankful to have met you! I'm currently on the train to Trieste, and I feel healed. The journal I am writing is actually an extended letter to a girl. I embarked on this journey because of her. I feel free and released. It doesn't matter where I go because I have already arrived," said Riko.

I felt my eyes getting warm. It brought me happiness knowing that Riko was able to continue his journey with a full heart and like me had started it with a broken one. The bus stopped rapidly. I moved my air pods from my ears.

"Salzburg!" announced the bus driver.

I got off the bus to grab my bags from underneath. My stomach started to sink. *Oh no, where are they?!* I thought. "Hello, do you speak English?" I asked.

The bus driver nodded his head. "I cannot find my bags!" I frantically looked around to make absolutely sure that I didn't spot them last minute.

The bus driver started moving bags. "We leave soon," he said.

"My bags must be here!" I pleaded. The other bus driver was motioning his hands for his coworker to get on the bus.

"Where did you put them?" he asked.

I could not remember which bin. He started opening up all of the bins, and I spotted my bag!

"You were not supposed to place it there!" he growled.

"I'm sorry!" I placed my hand over my heart. "Thank you," I said quickly. I grabbed my bags and made it just in time to get on the next bus to my hostel.

I walked into my hostel past midnight and checked in. "You'll be in room 236 with all girls," said the employee. I was relieved. I wanted to be with all girls. I opened the door and spotted two big blue eyes and three older men. I made one more look around the room turned around and wheeled my bag just as quickly as I had in.

"I paid extra to be with all girls," I said. The employee typed diligently on her computer and rolled her eyes. I felt good. I was finally starting to stand up for myself.

"You'll be in room 345," she responded quickly.

"Are you sure that is an all-girl room?" I asked.

She nodded her head and turned to speak to her other coworker.

I made it to my door and saw there was only one other girl staying in the room. I smiled from ear to ear and it was lights out.

I lifted my arms up and stretched. For the first time in a week I felt well rested. I went to the store to get a new SIM card that worked in Austria, Germany, and Hungary. I wanted to continue not being connected to the world during my travels but going through different countries made this difficult and within the next week I would be visiting three new countries! I realized how essential it was that I have google maps as I travel. In two days I would be going to the "Sound of Music" tour. A tour that my father and I had dreamed of doing together. *What should I wear?*

My palms were sweating as I looked through the clothes at H&M. I wanted to wear something special. I found the cutest two-piece dress that was a light color with flowers on it. *Dad would have loved this dress*, I thought. As I looked at the prices my shoulders sagged. It was thirty euros for the skirt and twenty euros for the shirt. *That's out of my budget*, I thought. I thought about my red dress that I had been saving for Egypt but realized that I was meant to wear this dress for the "Sound of Music" tour all along. This was the most beautiful dress I owned and the best dress I could wear when I showed my father pictures from the tour.

My father had always loved the *Sound of Music*. "You remind me of Maria," he'd say as he chuckled. I lifted my eyes and looked at him intently. "You are a free spirit, my dear daughter. I can't seem to pin you down."

Now here I was, about to attend the "Sound of Music" tour in Salzburg fifty years after it was created, and I felt nostalgic. *I need to go see the town,* I thought. I searched most popular view in Salzburg, which was the Hohensalzburg Fortress. *Thirty-two-minute walk from my hostel; not bad*, I thought.

I saw an older man walking with a cane with the help of his grandson. The view made me wish that my father was with me. I watched the grandson wrap his arm around his grandfather and hold him firmly. *I wish my father could be here with me right now*, I thought. I felt my eyes starting to get warm. *Stop that, Melissa. It's time to be happy*. I started snapping some photos to get my album ready to show my father.

I was rushing out the hostel at 4:00 am to catch my bus to Munich, Germany. I had always wanted to see Germany even if it cost me no sleep the night before. It was freezing outside. I started rubbing my hands together and heard a ding. *Great, the bus is running an hour late*, I thought. A lady approached me and started speaking to me in a different language. I shook my head. "I only speak English," I replied. I placed my hand on my heart and apologized. She mustered the courage to speak what English she could. "I have two little girls waiting for the bus in my car. Where do you go?" she asked. She waved her hand to signal that the girls were mid-size. *Probably teenagers*, I thought.

"I'm going to Munich," I responded.

"They are to meet their father. Can you look over them?" she asked. There was concern in her eyes. I nodded.

We got on the bus. One of the girls sat next to me, and the other girl sat three rows up as the bus was full. We approached border control and there were seven police officers. *This is intense*, I thought. The girl ahead of us kept turning her head to see if her sister was paying attention to the bus stops. I pulled up Google

Maps and notified the girl next to me how many minutes we had left. Here we were all different ages and I was looking out for these two as if they were my cubs. After all I gave their mother my word.

I got off the bus and found the first girl waiting for her sister then her sister approached after. "We don't know where our father is," one girl responded in broken English.

I wrapped my arm around her and said I'll be here until he arrives. Forty minutes later I saw two relieved smiles approach their faces as they ran into their father arms. He bowed and said, "Thank you." In English. I put my hand over my heart and bowed back. I turned around to start exploring the city!

I walked into Marianplatz and turned my head to take in each angle. My mouth opened wide as I noticed the intricate details that went into the architecture that lay in front of me. The city was busy and people were arm in arm laughing. I walked with my shoulders held high as I tried to soak in each view I could.

21

THE SOUND OF MUSIC

April 22, 2022

I hadn't done my makeup for weeks, but today was different—I could not wait to see my father's face when I showed him these pictures. I delicately put my red dress on and started to curl my hair. I played the *Sound of Music* soundtrack as I got ready. I walked to the tour two hours early to make sure that nothing could go wrong. I went to the café across the street and started to write; 1:45 pm approached quickly and I took a seat on the bus. "All aboard!" said the tour guide.

A few people in the crowd responded yes and nodded their heads. "Good because if you're not then we're leaving you here," said the tour guide. Laughter erupted and we were off. I looked out the window as my eyes started to burn. *I wish Dad could experience this with me*, I thought. I noticed a girl sitting by herself three rows up. We got out at the first stop and saw the house that the von Trapps had lived in.

"Are you alone too?" she asked. I nodded my head.

"What brings you here?" she asked.

I told her about my father and my solo travels. "What about you?" I asked.

"I've been traveling for a little over six months now. I grew up on the *Sound of Music* with my mother!" she replied.

We sat together for the rest of the tour and when the songs from *Sound of Music* started to play, we would sing. Something felt magical about this moment. We both connected in an instant notice over our love for the *Sound of Music* and I felt as if fate had placed us here so that we would be together. "Edelweiss" started playing on the bus and I had a flashback to the evenings my father would tuck me into bed and kiss me on the forehead and sing me this song. He had the most beautiful voice. *It is time to be happy*. I started to sing the way my father would sing, and a small smile came over my lips as I looked out the window.

I got my results of my Covid test, and it was negative. I started to pack my personal belongings and walked out of the hotel to take the metro to the airport to conclude my journey in Egypt. I realized it was Ramadan. Ramadan is the ninth month of the Islamic calendar, observed by Muslims worldwide as a month of fasting, prayer, reflection, and community. *What a perfect time to end my journey in Egypt*, I thought. I looked at my phone and realized today was the first day that Sam hadn't texted me. I called Ann.

"Maybe he's busy. You should just text him to see what's wrong," she said.

I thought about this and before I knew it the words came tumbling out of my mouth. "I'm done putting in extra effort into a man who is not reciprocating. I know my self-worth and I am not willing to settle!" I responded.

It was just as beautiful as I had imagined. I looked at the Great Pyramid of Giza in admiration. I was taught that there is a logical reason for everything that happens. As I stared at the Great Pyramid of Giza, I continued to wonder how this masterpiece could have been built in roughly 2570 BC. *It is humanly impossible*, I thought. I realized in this moment that sometimes there is not an answer. Sometimes it's okay to accept what is.

"How do you think the pyramids were built?" asked my tour guide.

"Isn't that the magic question?" I responded. I looked at every stone, and it reminded me of myself. Every piece of my story that made me into the masterpiece that I am today. *It's time to do something adventurous*, I thought. I had a white shirt that had Justin's picture on the back of it and knew that I wanted to wear it on the perfect occasion. *What better occasion than going on an ATV in the Egyptian desert?* I thought.

I walked toward the entrance of my hotel to meet my tour guide. Today Justin was going to experience the Egyptian desert with me. I needed his spirit in order to get on an ATV for my first time.

"This is how you start and stop," said the tour guide. I swung my leg over the seat and got prepared. I felt a warm breeze hit my shoulder. It felt as if someone had just nudged me to go. I looked up toward the sky and saw a bird flying. My lips moved up as my eyes stung. I kissed my finger and lifted it up to the sky.

"I love you J," I said out loud as I started the ATV. I felt as if I was one with the ATV. Riding quickly and fearlessly in the Arabian Desert.

The Alchemist originally inspired me to go to Egypt. I opened *The Alchemist* for the first time this trip. I couldn't let go of the book. Each page had a new meaning to me that I hadn't appreciated before. I felt the words singing to me with pain and happiness all at the same time. When I got to the last page, I noticed a note at the end of the book that I had never realized before. A note in Spanish from Carlos and Lorena that thanked my father for his kindness and heart.

"Would you like to go to dinner with me this evening?" asked the handsome man.

I started fidgeting my fingers. "I have an early flight tomorrow," I responded.

The man smiled. "I understand," he said as he turned around slowly and started to walk away.

"Wait!" I said, startled by my own reaction.

The man looked surprised. "I would like to accompany you for dinner," I responded.

We met at 7:00 pm. "Can I get you a drink?" asked the waiter.

"Can I have a Coca Cola, please," I said.

"You don't want a drink?" asked the man.

"I'm not drinking tonight," I responded as I gave him a smile.

"So tell me what brought you to Egypt?" asked the man.

"It's a long story," I said.

"I have time," said the man.

I felt confident, strong, and beautiful. I moved my right arm out and opened it up.

"Well… It all started when…"

22

THE MOMENT I KNEW I WAS READY TO COME HOME

I started packing my final things to head home to the United States. I shuffled through my backpack and grabbed my Ativan and Adderall bottle and walked to the bathroom. I opened both bottles and poured the pills into my left hand. The blue and white pills spread out throughout my palm—these pills were a constant reminder of the times I took them to make it through the day. I spent several seconds looking at my hand—having rapid flashbacks of some of my worse memories in the past. I flipped my hand over quickly as I heard multiple droplets.

"Are you ready to do this?" I asked myself out loud, fully knowing the answer to my question.

I used my right hand to flush the toilet and watched the toilet swirl in a circular motion until half the pills were gone. I flushed one more time and watched the rest of the pills descend into the endless sewer line that was underneath the Nine Pyramids View Hotel in Cairo, Egypt. I knew I was ready to come home.

As I walked to my gate I pulled out my phone. *It's time to block Bradley's phone number*, I thought. I typed in Bradley's name in contacts then selected "Block This Caller." I started to smile from ear to ear. I stood up with my chin held high.

"Now I'm ready to come back home."

When I started this journey I knew I wasn't myself anymore. I felt like a mirror that could break at any moment and that I would shatter into a million pieces. I was weak and I felt broken. I didn't realize how much hatred I felt toward myself for that fateful evening I was sexually assaulted and the way I handled it afterwards.

I continued to ask myself the same eight questions. *Why was an unnecessary surgery recommended to my father? Why was I sexually assaulted? Why did I continue to pursue the person who had sexually assaulted me? Why didn't my manager protect me? Why didn't my company protect me? Why didn't this individual get held accountable when he yelled sexually explicit comments at a company-sponsored event? Why did my boyfriend cheat on me?* and *Why did my dear childhood friend pass away?* I was worried these questions would consume my mind until I drove myself crazy. What I realized at the end of my trip is that I can never turn back the clock to rewind these events. I realized through this trip that I had stopped asking myself the same questions that circled my mind endlessly, and I found what inner peace felt like again. *What would Dad think?* I thought as I looked out the window—my lips raised up. *He would be so proud of me.*

I traveled through Spain, Italy, France, Portugal, San Marino,

Albania, North Macedonia, Montenegro, Croatia, Slovenia, Austria, Germany, Hungary, Slovakia, and Egypt. During my trip I started to fall back in love with myself. When I look in the mirror I see each battle wound I carry. Every tear and anxiety attack I experienced. Each choice and decision I've made that has shaped me into the woman I am today. After three and a half months of traveling I held my head up high as I walked to the gate to go back home.

I spent most of my savings on my journey. "Have you gone mad?" one of my friends asked.

"Maybe." I paused. "But I would rather have peace with no money than be miserable with lots of money," I responded.

I needed to complete this journey across the world to find inner peace. I had to go through loneliness, adventure, and the unknown to discover what was waiting for me all along. Every one of us has a treasure that awaits them. Listen to your heart. When you listen to your heart, you will find your true calling and ultimately the biggest treasure. My question for you is: What are you willing to risk to get it?

I learned through my trip that I am strong, I am powerful, and most importantly I learned that I can protect myself. I am able to share my story in hopes that it helps another woman in the world. What I realized is that I've had the power within me all along even if I didn't see it until now. "The truth shall set you free. No matter how painful or difficult your truth may be," said my father. The relationship I had with my father is one that I will treasure forever. I will hold onto what my father taught me. After all, I am my father's daughter.

23

THE LAST CONVERSATION
I HAD WITH MY DAD WHERE HE
WAS COHERENT

It was a cold day in April 2018 when I visited my father at our childhood home—this was the last time I saw him when he had his full mental capacity. "As you go through life you will learn that your words and your actions are two of the most powerful things you have. Life isn't fair. Bad things happen to good people. I hope if I teach you anything it is to use your words to influence change," said my father.

"I will, Dad! I learned from the best," I responded.

"Melissa, I want you to make me one promise. I will not be here forever. I know that's hard to believe but I want you to remember this. Give me your word that you will not forget what I am about to ask you," said my father.

I nodded my head as our eyes locked.

"What I am about to ask you is one of my dreams. When I am gone,

I want this dream to live on through me, and I know the only way this can happen is through you," said my father.

I continued to look at my father's piercing blue eyes and I could tell the seriousness he had.

"Promise me that whenever you have extra money from my rental income you use it to build a small home for a family in need within your mother's homeland of Dominican Republic. My dream is for you to establish multiple homes," said my father.

"You have my word," I responded. I remember this conversation vividly. It brings me back to that warm sunny day where I felt like I would have my father forever.

My father paused as he shook his finger slowly while he moved his finger up down.

"One more thing," said my father. My father put his arm around my shoulders and I saw his lips rise. "Out of all the things I have accomplished in my life, my biggest accomplishment was being your father."

24

LEARNINGS FROM DAD, SUMMED UP IN A LIST OF TEN

1. It's what in your heart that matters
2. Do what you love, the money will follow
3. Stand up for what you believe in—no matter the cost
4. Help others whenever you can
5. Be kind
6. Be honest
7. Be loyal
8. Actions speak louder than words
9. Your character and integrity mean everything
10. You can make a difference. Never lose faith in that.

25

LETTER TO CHAD CUNNINGHAM

n April 20, 2018, you performed an invasive operation on my father. This may be another statistic for you—and another paycheck. For me, I lost my father mentally. Shortly after you performed surgery my father was unable to speak, eat, or walk. My father was bedridden for seven months while my family searched for answers to get my father help.

I attempted to call your office on many occasions and heard crickets. On the afternoon that you returned my call (6 months later) I got 35 minutes of your time. Thirty-five minutes in which you demonstrated no empathy or care.

In June 2018 I proudly graduated from Portland State University. Under normal circumstances my family would have been there to help me celebrate this achievement. As it was, my family was unable to attend due to my father's declining health and his need for constant care. The feeling of loss I felt as I gazed upon the empty chairs highlighted the pivotal role my dad played in maintaining the stability of my family, as well as my own personal sense of grounding. My dad was an invaluable contributor in my life, and in the life of countless others. He was the foundational rock of our family unit, and a value added member to each community he served.

On May 31, 2021, when I was in mediation I was shocked to find out that the defense team's main argument was that you should have never completed surgery on my father. Unbeknownst to me one of your fellow peers in Medford said, "Your father was too high functioning to receive this surgery."

The deterioration of my dad's physical and mental health that occurred as a result of you performing an unnecessary surgery has left him a hollow shell of the man he once was. While my dad is indeed psychically alive today, he has in fact essentially lost his life. If one were to look upon this once strong and capable man, they would now see a person incapable of normal communication, unable to smile, laugh or even articulate what his basic human needs are.

My family and I are left feeling unable to help the man who helped so many others. This has been a long ordeal (one that I pray no family ever goes through). My father was not only a hero to me but to many people he crossed paths with. He always wanted to help anyone that he met. My dad did not deserve this.

You took an oath to serve your clients interest the day you became a neurosurgeon. As you think of that oath, please take time to think about the patients you serve. Think about their family members that love them. You are directly impacting each life the moment you start performing a surgery.

26

LETTER TO BRADLEY MORRISON

The night you sexually assaulted me you took a piece of me that I thought I would never get back. For years I searched for inner peace. I tried to justify what you did. *Maybe he was just drunk,* I thought. I tried to pursue a relationship with you. *Maybe that would make me feel better*, I thought. When I looked in the mirror, I looked at myself with disgust. I felt gross in my own skin. *How could anyone want to be with me?* I thought. As tears poured down my cheeks I would wipe them away and grab my clothes to get started with the day. I had a constant reminder of that fateful evening each morning I drove to work. My throat would choke up and I continued to ask myself two questions: "Will I ever be happy again?" and "Will I ever love myself again?"

What I realized through my trip is that this day doesn't need to define me. I don't have to feel embarrassed, gross, or anything "less than" when I look at myself in the mirror. The last night I saw you, on November 6, 2021, you told me that I should thank you. I would like to thank you. If you hadn't sexually assaulted me, I wouldn't be the woman I am today, and I would have never realized my inner strength. I would have continued to work in a job that did not bring me true happiness or meaning. I would have never discovered my passion, which is to write. I hope this experience helps you realize that your actions can play a critical role in someone else's life. Your drug of choice, alcohol, can impact a decision you may not make when sober. I hope this event changes you and your future decisions in how you will treat women. This experience has made me realize I am capable of standing up for myself.

27

THE NEW EQUILIBRIUM

Lily made her way back to the Netherlands with Teuntje and arrived at her family's home on April 20, 2022. After Lily's brother passed she'd stopped caring about what other people thought of her.

"I'm sad that it took my brother passing to realize this but I firmly believe that you should live the life that makes you happy without caring what others think," said Lily. Lily is currently working on building her own you tube channel and is planning her next big trip. Lily's dream is to open her own business to help create a more sustainable future.

My mother called me and her voice had a skip in it. "I need you to drive to Medford. Your father is okay, but I found out the property management company was committing fraud," said my mother.

I arrived in the United States on May 3, 2022. Alice was waiting in her Subaru and I ran into her arms. Alice rubbed my back and I looked into her eyes. "It's good to have you home," said Alice. I carried my suitcases up the carpeted floors and let them go as my shoulders fell to the ground. I took a deep breath in and out and observed my room that looked untouched just the way I had left it.

I woke up and gathered a few last minute items to head to my hometown of Medford. The sun was beaming, and in four hours I would be running into my mother's and father's arms. I drove up the driveway and saw my childhood home to the right. The grass was long and unkempt, the trees were overarching the property. I used my left hand to swing the driver door open and leaped to my parents' front door. I used my finger to punch the doorbell twice.

My father opened the door and was bent over. He moved his head up slowly and his eyes grew wider. I ran into his arms. He stumbled a few feet backwards and I held his back delicately with my left arm. My father took seven steps to the couch and sat down. I laid my head on his shoulder and hugged him tightly. My father smiled from ear to ear as he patted my shoulder.

My mother walked down the stairs, and I ran into her arms. She rubbed my hair with her right fingertips. I looked into my mother's eyes and saw determination. In an hour and a half we would be meeting two of the representatives that worked for the property management company at a property that my parents owned.

I drove my mother to the property and saw that the owner and his employee were already there. I swung the door open and ran to the other side to open the door for my mother. The owner of the management company walked toward me and kept his eyes on the ground. He was fidgeting with his hands.

"I am looking forwards to seeing the remodel," I said. I took the spare key and opened the door. When I walked inside the floor looked rusty. The walls had unfinished paint and the appliances were old. "You charged my mother and father thousands of dollars for what?" I asked. I stabilized my voice and continued to try to make eye contact with the owner as he looked down.

"The place was left in poor condition. We were not done but your mother continued to want to see the place," he responded quickly. My mother noticed a recurring theme that her rental units were not receiving the work the property management company claimed to be doing.

The owner of the property management company made eye contact with me for the first time. "If you are not happy with the work, we will wire you the money we charged because that is the type of company we are."

My mother was furious. "Your men did not do anything! How can you charge us thousands of dollars for this?! Of course you have to send our money back." She rubbed her eyes quickly with the palm of her hand.

I rubbed my mother's shoulders and continued to look around the unit in shock. *How many times have they taken advantage of my parents?* I thought.

It was in this moment I knew it was time to help my mother manage the properties. I drafted new lease agreements, and effective June 1, 2022, my mother and I would be managing my parents' properties. On May 22, 2022, my father and I started visiting the rentals. As I knocked on the door I had a flashback to when I was a child in my father's truck, watching him stride up the stairs and bang on the door three times. As the door opened I started speaking to one of my father's tenants and I smiled from ear to ear.

A tenant walked to the car and I opened the passenger door so she could say hello to my father. "James, you changed my life. I don't know if you remember this but you bought my son an Xbox twenty years ago. He is now thirty-four years old and will never get rid of his Xbox," she said. She wiped a tear from her cheek and continued to look at my father. My father looked toward the ground and nodded his head slowly.

She reached for my shoulder and squeezed it. "You have a special father," she said. I looked at her as tears approached my eyes and nodded my head.

"You'll be seeing us a lot more often!" I responded as I grabbed the handle and sat in the driver's seat. I waved goodbye and started the car. I looked toward my father and saw a small smile appear from his lips. It was around lunch time and I heard my father's stomach growl. I approached Taco Bell. I asked my father what he would like. I waited patiently and heard a small voice.

"A number seven, please," said my father.

We were at the same Taco Bell where I started my first job when I was sixteen years old. I reached for my father's hand; he looked into my eyes and scrunched his face. "I would like to hold your hand if that is okay," I said. I opened my palm and my father moved his left hand toward it slowly. I squeezed his hand gently and searched for Karen Carpenter on Spotify.

My father started lip-syncing "Yesterday Once More." I saw a small tear fall down his cheek bone. I pulled my car over to introduce myself to the next tenant as my father watched me from the passenger side window.

I relocated to Medford and started managing the rentals with my mother. I heard someone call us the "dynamic Work duo." My father was not vocal but observant. I noticed a smile from time to time which provided me comfort knowing that my father would be proud.

After my trip, my mindset had shifted. I was able to read and understand people better. I did not care what people thought about me, and my priorities changed. I started to see life in a unique perspective and realized what was important to me. I never thought I would want to move back home. I realized after my trip that being with my family brought me great happiness. There was no other place I would rather be than home. As I knocked on tenants' doors, I smiled ear to ear hearing their stories about my father and knowing that my father did the same thing I was doing years ago.

"I was wondering if you could throw away these branches and trash?" asked a tenant.

I nodded my head. "Looks like it will be one dump run. I'll be here in the morning with the truck," I responded. I turned around to see my father looking at me through the passenger side window and saw a smile appear from his lips.

I rubbed my father's leg. "You ready to play some cards?!" I asked. My father nodded his head slowly.

In lives ever changing, some things stay the same.

www.ingramcontent.com/pod-product-compliance
Lightning Source LLC
Chambersburg PA
CBHW031500160726
47994CB00005B/2124